■■SCHOLASTIC

Kid Scoop®

Independent Activity Pages for Reading
Kids Can't Resist!

By Vicki Whiting
From the popular Kid Scoop®
newspaper feature!

NEW YORK • TORONTO • LONDON • AUCKLAND • SYDNEY **Teaching** *Resources*
MEXICO CITY • NEW DELHI • HONG KONG • BUENOS AIRES

Cover design by Maria Lilja
Interior design by Jeff Schinkel and Dawn Armato-Brehm

ISBN: 0-439-51776-1
Copyright © 2004 by Vicki Whiting.
Published by Scholastic Inc.
All rights reserved
Printed in the U.S.A.

Table of Contents

When lessons are "super fun," they also provide super serious learning! Kid Scoop's weekly newspaper feature has engaged students and teachers alike for more than 10 years. Now the pencil-grabbing puzzles and standards-based, kid-friendly stories are collected into one book, providing you and your students with a year's worth of fun at your fingertips.

Each topic is provided as a two-page spread. Copy on two sides of one sheet of paper or on two separate pages. You can use the pages in the order suggested here, or in any order that fits your curriculum.

Name_____ Date _____

Johnny Appleseed:
A Gentle Hero

Johnny Appleseed was born in Leominster, Massachusetts, on September 26, 1774. His real name was John Chapman.

Johnny Appleseed got his name because of the role he played in planting apple trees in the midwestern part of the United States.

In the late 1700s, the United States government granted land to people who would start farms. In order to keep the land, settlers had to show that they were going to stay and farm. One of the rules was that a settler had to plant 50 apple trees.

Johnny Appleseed saw that there was a need to supply seeds and seedlings to the settlers. He traveled west ahead of the pioneers and started apple nurseries throughout what is now Ohio and Indiana.

Help Johnny Appleseed find his way to each of the settler's farms.

Standards Link Physical Education: Eye Hand Coordination; Mathematical Reasoning: Problem Solving.

START

Legend claims that Johnny Appleseed once saved a wolf from a trap and that the wolf then traveled with Johnny and his old horse.

Perhaps it was his gentle spirit that made Johnny Appleseed an American legend. Known as a loving, caring man, he was accepted as a peacemaker between Native Americans and settlers.

Over the years, stories grew out of the sketchy historical facts, and John "Johnny Appleseed" Chapman became an American folk hero.

Standards Link History: Students Understand the Importance of Individual Action and Character and Explain How Heroes from Long Ago Made a Difference in Our Lives Today.

What can a whole apple do that a half apple can't?

ANSWER: It can look round.

Name_____   Date _____

Add Up the Apples

Can you find where each apple came from on the tree? The numbers match and so do the shapes!

3+8=

4+5=

7+6=

3+2=

6+4=

13   11   5

9   10

Standards Link Math: Compute Sums to 20.

Awesome Apples

Find the two apples that are alike.

Standards Link Scientific Investigation and Observation: Identify Similarities and Differences in Common Objects.

Scrambled A's

How many times is the letter "A" written below?

Standards Link Language Arts/Reading: Phonemic Awareness, Decoding.

Double Double Word Search

Find the words in the puzzle, then in the Kid Scoop stories and activities.

S	E	I	R	O	T	S	J	D	S
H	G	E	N	T	L	E	E	W	R
O	E	O	H	N	T	E	N	O	E
R	Y	R	F	L	S	R	A	L	L
S	P	A	O	E	P	T	A	F	T
E	R	I	L	G	R	E	W	P	T
M	H	P	K	E	L	E	S	E	E
O	P	Y	N	N	H	O	J	E	S
A	L	A	N	D	D	N	O	W	K

JOHNNY   GREW
TREES   STORIES
FOLK   TRAP
HERO   SETTLERS
LEGEND   WOLF
APPLESEED   HORSE
FARM   OHIO
GENTLE   LAND

Standards Link Language Arts: Spelling: Letter Sequencing; Reading: Vocabulary Development: Recognize Identical Words.

Alpacas

What am I?

I am related to a camel, but I am much fuzzier. I "talk" to others of my kind by making bugling, clucking, and humming sounds. My fur is so soft that Inca kings and queens used it for their royal robes.

The Alpaca

Most alpacas live in Peru, which is a country in South America. Alpacas live high in the mountains where it is very cold. They have soft, warm fur to keep warm.

Their fur is what has made alpacas important animals to many South American families. They raise alpacas for this soft and beautiful fur. South American families have been raising alpacas for more than 6,000 years. The alpaca can be a favorite family pet as well as a way to earn money from the sale of its valuable fur.

COLOMBIA
ECUADOR
BRAZIL
P E R U
Pacific Ocean
CHILE

Not Just South America Any More

Alpacas were first brought to the United States in 1984. Now families in the U.S. raise alpacas for their fur and as pets. Today there are about 10,000 alpacas in the United States. There are about 3,000,000 in Peru.

Standards Link Science: Animals Have Features that Serve Different Functions in Growth and Survival.

Start

Paca Puzzle

Find your way through the alpaca's fur.

Standards Link Physical Education: Eye Hand Coordination; Math Reasoning: Problem Solving.

Finish

Use the code to discover some alpaca facts.

Alpaca fur comes in 🌴🌴 colors.

Alpacas can live for 🌴☀ or more years.

Alpacas grow to about ◨◖ inches tall at the withers (shoulders) and weigh about 🔺⭐☀ pounds.

☀	🔺	🌴	◨	👕	⭐	◖	⬡	⊟	⫽
0	1	2	3	4	5	6	7	8	9

Standards Link Reading Comprehension: Follow Simple Written Directions.

What has four LEGS, a BACK, and no BODY?

ANSWER: A chair.

Name_____ Date _____

Famous Fur

Sweaters made from alpaca fur are famous for being soft and warm. Number the pictures from 1 to 4 to show how fur from an alpaca becomes a sweater.

1. Alpacas get a haircut once a year. It takes about 20 minutes to cut off or "shear" one alpaca. The fur that is sheared off is called "fleece."

2. The fleece is cleaned with a special brush. Brushing alpaca fleece is also called "carding."

3. Spinners turn the brushed fur, called "fiber," into yarn.

4. The yarn is then used to make sweaters and other products.

Standards Link Reading Comprehension: Students Read from a Variety of Genres Including Non Fiction.

Is an alpaca the same as a llama?

No way!

An alpaca and a llama are in the same family, like a zebra and a horse. But they are different, just as you may be quite different from your cousin.

An alpaca is smaller than a llama. A llama is more than two times as large as an alpaca. Alpacas are raised for their fine fur, while the llama is mostly used as a pack animal. And alpacas are generally more sweet-tempered than llamas.

Standards Link Science: Animals Have External Features that Vary from Related Species.

Kid Scoop thanks the Alpaca Owners and Breeders Association for their help with this page. You can contact them for more information about alpacas by calling 1-800-213-9522 or going to **www.alpacainfo.com**

Double Double Word Search

Find the words in the puzzle, then in the Kid Scoop stories and activities.

A	L	P	R	O	W	S	T	E	P
S	O	U	T	H	Y	A	S	L	C
R	A	A	L	C	R	R	R	E	A
E	R	C	E	S	O	C	E	M	R
H	N	T	A	H	Y	R	A	A	D
T	U	R	E	P	A	L	U	C	I
I	E	C	E	E	L	F	L	F	N
W	I	W	H	E	W	A	D	O	G
C	U	S	G	W	P	S	A	L	P

ALPACAS	WITHERS
PERU	SHEAR
ROYAL	HORSE
FLEECE	PETS
LLAMA	SOUTH
SWEET	FUR
WARM	CAMEL
CARDING	

Standards Link Language Arts: Spelling: Letter Sequencing; Reading: Vocabulary Development: Recognize Identical Words.

Name_____ Date_____

Kid Scoop® Backpacks

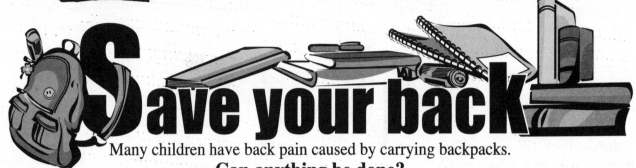

Save your back

Many children have back pain caused by carrying backpacks.
Can anything be done?

SPOT THE BACKPACK BLUNDERS

Sophia Softshoulders has the latest, greatest backpack. But it is doing her no good. She is wearing it all wrong!

Find the differences between Sophia's before-and-after pictures. Read how to BE A BACKPACK MASTER and put an "X" on each of the five backpack blunders.

Before | **After**

Standards Link Science: Recognize Similarities and Differences in Common Objects Through Observation.

DOCTOR'S SOLUTION

The solution most doctors recommend is to wear the backpack correctly and lighten the load!

HOW MUCH CAN YOU CARRY?

A healthy rule of thumb is to carry only 10% of your body weight.	If you weigh:	Your backpack shouldn't weigh more than:
	50 lbs.	5 lbs.
	60 lbs.	6 lbs.
	70 lbs.	7 lbs.
	80 lbs.	8 lbs.
	90 lbs.	9 lbs.
	100 lbs.	10 lbs.
	110 lbs.	11 lbs.

Sam weighs 70 pounds.
Anna weighs 90 pounds.
Circle in red the things that Sam could carry. Circle in green the things that Anna could carry.

history book	2 lbs.
paperback novel	1/2 lbs. (8 oz)
two folders	1/4 lbs. (4 oz)
pencil bag	1/4 lbs. (4 oz)
wallet	1/4 lbs. (4 oz)
newspaper	1/4 lbs. (4 oz)
lunch	1 lbs.
binder	2 lbs.
dictionary	3 lbs.
math book	2 lbs.

Standards Link Math: Measure Using Standard Units; Compute Sums.

WHAT IS THE STRONGEST ANIMAL?

ANSWER: The snail. It carries its house on its back.

Name_____ Date _____

BE A BACKPACK MASTER

Backpacks are still a good way to carry heavy loads.
The trick is to know how to wear a backpack the right way.

☐ Wear both shoulder straps. This spreads the load of school supplies evenly across your back.

☐ Use the waist belt.

☐ Use the side/chest straps.

☐ Tighten shoulder straps so the pack fits close to the upper part of your back.

☐ Load the pack with the heaviest items right next to your back.

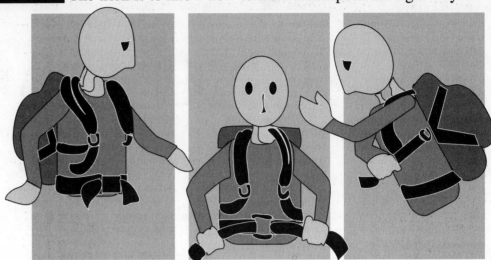

Source: Consumer Reports for Kids www.zillions.org/Features/Backpacks/backpack002.html

Standards Link Health: Students Make Decisions That Maintain and Enhance Health.

What's in Silly Sam's Backpack?

Make sure that you're not lugging around stuff that you don't need in your backpack. Silly Sam needs to unload some extra weight from his pack. To Þnd out what it is, color in the spaces with one dot.

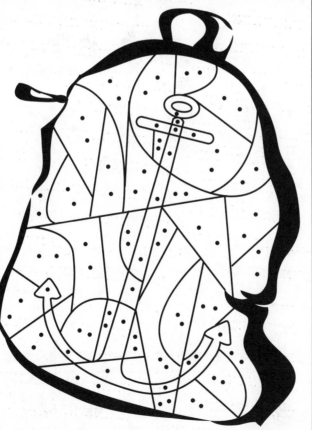

Standards Link Reading Comprehension: Follow Simple Written Directions.

Double Double Word Search

Find the words in the puzzle, then in the Kid Scoop stories and activities.

S	U	S	I	G	N	O	R	W	K
A	N	T	V	T	E	Y	O	S	B
B	L	U	N	D	E	R	S	A	S
R	O	F	O	U	D	M	C	V	T
E	A	F	R	B	A	K	S	E	R
T	D	N	U	O	P	M	O	C	A
S	T	S	I	A	W	N	I	A	P
A	C	K	C	W	E	I	G	H	S
M	N	K	O	Y	R	R	A	C	W

BACKPACK   WRONG
BLUNDERS   WEIGH
STRAPS   MASTER
WAIST   CARRY
UNLOAD   STUFF
ITEMS   PAIN

Standards Link Language Arts: Spelling: Letter Sequencing; Reading: Vocabulary Development: Recognize Identical Words.

Name_____ Date _____

Kid Scoop — Sign Language

TALKING HANDS

Find which trail points all the way to the finish.

Standards Link: Reading Comprehension: Follow simple directions; eye-hand coordination.

Some people talk with their hands. This is called **sign language**.

Sign language is useful for people who cannot hear, but can see. They can see words made by people's hands and talk back with words using their own hands.

Standards Link Reading Comprehension: Students Identify Basic Facts and Ideas In What They Read; Use Illustrations to Understand Meaning.

American Manual Alphabet

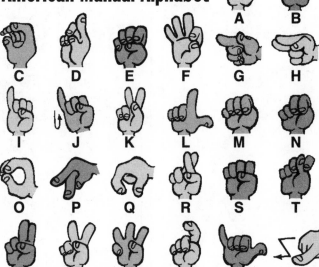

A B C D E F G H I J K L M N O P Q R S T U V W X Y Z

Learn Sign Language

You can talk in sign language in two different ways. One way is to spell words, letter by letter, using the American Manual Alphabet. The other way is to make special hand motions that mean one word or a group of words. This is called "signing a word."

Here is the way to spell the word **"eat"** in the American Manual Alphabet:

E A T

Here is how you sign the word **"eat"**:

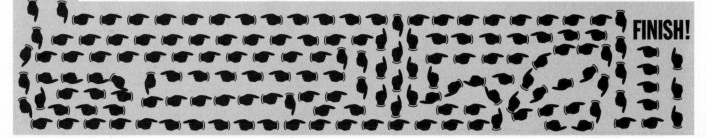

FINISH!

My dad is so strong he can hold up 10 **CARS** and a **TRUCK** with one hand!

He must be the world's greatest weightlifter!

Nope, he's a traffic cop!

Name_____ Date _____

Draw a line from each picture to the American Manual Alphabet spelling for the name of the picture.

Standards Link Reading Comprehension: Follow Simple Directions; Identify Letters; Read Common Sight Words.

Silly Signing

Q: **What do you get when you cross a turtle and a porcupine?**

Use sign language to discover the answer.

Standards Link Reading Comprehension: Follow Simple One-step Directions.

Double Double Word Search

Find the words in the puzzle, then in the Kid Scoop stories and activities.

S	G	L	K	D	S	G	M	A	U
I	L	E	T	T	E	R	O	L	G
S	T	A	L	K	M	O	T	P	F
P	R	T	N	N	A	U	I	H	R
E	N	S	I	G	N	P	O	A	I
C	M	P	T	T	U	H	N	B	E
I	H	E	A	R	A	A	S	E	N
A	F	L	S	U	L	N	G	T	D
L	D	L	W	O	R	D	S	E	M
U	S	E	F	U	L	S	T	T	R

SIGN   WORDS
TALK   LETTER
LANGUAGE   SPECIAL
HANDS   USEFUL
SPELL   EAT
MANUAL   HEAR
MOTIONS   GROUP

Standards Link Language Arts: Spelling: Letter Sequencing; Reading: Vocabulary Development: Recognize Identical Words.

Kid Scoop® — Snowy Owls

The Snowy Owl

Like a ghost, the snowy owl glides through the air in soundless flight. This owl is different from most owls because it hunts during the day and at night. Most owls hunt at night. In the arctic region, the summer days and nights are always light. An owl waiting for darkness to hunt would starve before the dark days of winter arrive.

Connect the dots to draw a snowy owl in flight.

Why White?

Many animals can blend into their environment. This is called camouflage. There are few trees on the tundra, so the snowy owl's white plumage blends with the snowy world of the northern arctic.

In the spring, when the snowy owl makes a nest, the snow has started to melt and the brown earth shows through patches of white snow. The female snowy owl's soft white feathers are streaked with brown so she cannot be seen as she nests on the ground.

Here are three other animals that blend into their "habitats," or homes. Can you unscramble their names?

**POLEDAR
REDE
EGIRT**

Standards Link Science: Animals Have External Features that Help Them Thrive in the Different Environments They Inhabit.

How big is a snowy owl?

The snowy owl is one of the largest owls, with a height of about 27 inches (69 cm) and a wingspan of up to 60 inches (152 cm). Wingspan is the measurement from wing tip to wing tip, when the wings are fully stretched.

How many of the things in this chart could fit into a snowy owl's wingspan?

Microwave oven	25 inches (63.5 cm)
Teacher's desk	40 inches (102 cm)
House cat	25 inches (63.5 cm)
Baseball bat	33 inches (84 cm)
Tennis racket	27 inches (69 cm)
Small car (width)	67 inches (170 cm)

Measure 60 inches (152 cm) on the floor. Now lie down with your arms outstretched along the line. Measure your outstretched arms. How do you compare?

Standards Link Math: Measurement: Student Compare the Length of Objects by Using Direct Comparison of Standard and Non Standard Units.

Baby owls are called owlets. Can you help the mother owl find her way home to her owlets?

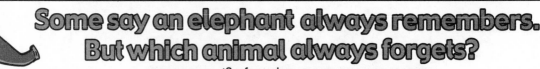

Some say an elephant always remembers. But which animal always forgets?

ANSWER: The owl. It keeps saying, "Who? Who?"

Name_____   Date_____

Owl Eyes

All owls have excellent sight so that they can spot creatures like mice that run fast along the ground. Owls' eyes are not the same as human eyes. We move our eyes in their sockets to see from side to side. The owl must turn his head to see in different directions. Owls also have a third eyelid, which protects the eye. It is a milky white eyelid that comes up from the bottom of the eye. Its purpose is to clean and refresh the owl's eyes. This third eyelid is called a *nictitating membrane*.

Standards Link Science: Adaptations in Physical Structures Improve an Animal's Chance for Survival.

The Eyes Have It

The snowy owl has round, yellow eyes. Can you find the pairs of eyes that match?

Standard Links Scientific Investigation: Identify Similarities and Differences in Common Objects.

Don't chew your food, dear. Swallow it whole.

Snowy owls need to eat a huge amount each day— enough to equal their own body weight. They don't chew their food—they just swallow their prey whole, including fur, claws, teeth, and bones. Then they spit out a pellet of all the parts they can't digest.

What silly things can you find on this owl's dinner plate?

Standards Link Science: Animals Need Food for Survival and Have Physical Structures to Help Them Survive.

Double Double Word Search

Find the words in the puzzle, then in the Kid Scoop stories and activities.

Y	L	O	W	G	P	S	A	B	P
M	E	M	T	O	W	R	O	D	M
E	T	H	G	I	S	N	E	L	E
G	T	O	B	L	E	N	D	Y	M
A	N	A	P	S	G	N	I	W	B
M	U	P	O	S	B	L	G	O	R
U	O	C	H	E	W	R	E	N	A
L	C	T	S	O	H	G	S	S	N
P	C	A	R	D	N	U	T	W	E

SNOWY   SPOT
OWL   SIGHT
WINGSPAN   CHEW
MEMBRANE   PREY
DIGEST   BLEND
BONES   GHOST
TUNDRA   PLUMAGE

Standards Link Language Arts: Spelling: Letter Sequencing; Reading: Vocabulary Development: Recognize Identical Words.

Kid Scoop — Strange ... But True

STRANGE ...But True!

Whoever says truth can be stranger than fiction must have studied some of the earth's unusual and fascinating animals!

Birds Build Apartment House

On the dry, flat African plains, weaverbirds live in large colonies of 30 or more pairs. They work together to build one large nest for the entire colony. It is a bird apartment house and each pair of birds has its own "apartment," or nesting room.

The nests are made of straw and grass, and they are often made in the thorny branches of an acacia tree.

Standards Link Science: Diverse Life Forms Live and Adapt to Different Environments.

Help the mother weaverbird find her nesting room.

HOME

START

Nest Facts

Some nests are ▼❱ feet tall and ▼★ feet wide. Nests have been found with more than ▼★★ weaverbird families!

NEST CODE:
★ =0   ▼ =1   ❱ =5

Creature Survives Four Years Without Food or Water

African lungfish live in swampy places. During the dry season, the water disappears for a time. The amazing lungfish has found a way to adapt.

It folds its 6-foot-long body into a U shape with its head and tail pointing upward. Its skin makes a thin mucus covering that protects the fish from drying out. When the water disappears and the fish finds itself covered in hard-baked mud, it goes into a state of deep sleep called "estivation," which is a kind of hot-season hibernation.

The lungfish remains like this until rain comes and softens the mud. In times of drought it can take years for the rains to return. No problem! The lungfish can live like this for four years.

Standards Link Science: Animals Adapt to Their Environment.

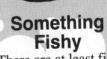
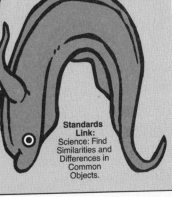

Something Fishy

There are at least five differences between these two lungfish. Can you find them all?

Standards Link: Science: Find Similarities and Differences in Common Objects.

What animal doesn't play fair?

ANSWER: The cheetah.

Name_____ Date _____

If It Moves, It's Mother!

A gosling is a baby goose. After hatching, the greylag gosling will follow the first moving object it sees. It thinks whatever moves is its mother! In fact, goslings have adopted several very different "mothers."

Circle every item in the puzzle that appears two times. These are some of the different things goslings adopted as "mothers."

Standards Link Science: Animals Have Different Strategies for Growth and Survival.

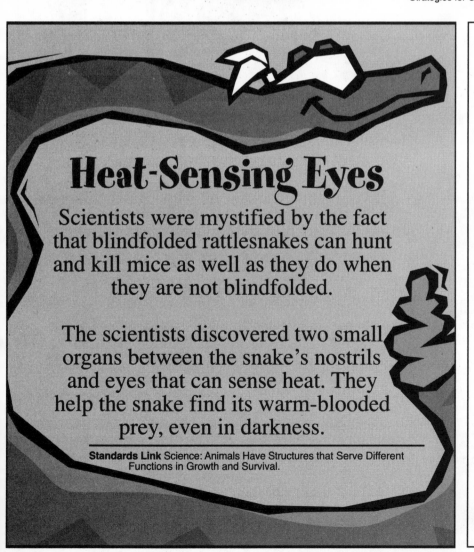

Heat-Sensing Eyes

Scientists were mystified by the fact that blindfolded rattlesnakes can hunt and kill mice as well as they do when they are not blindfolded.

The scientists discovered two small organs between the snake's nostrils and eyes that can sense heat. They help the snake find its warm-blooded prey, even in darkness.

Standards Link Science: Animals Have Structures that Serve Different Functions in Growth and Survival.

Double Double Word Search

Find the words in the puzzle, then in the Kid Scoop stories and activities.

I	N	C	P	R	E	Y	E	R	P
Y	E	A	L	S	D	N	I	B	E
N	I	G	U	T	H	O	L	K	E
R	E	O	N	R	T	L	C	A	L
O	S	S	G	A	U	O	N	D	S
H	S	L	F	W	R	C	A	M	A
T	A	I	I	Z	T	T	A	E	H
I	R	N	S	N	G	F	S	A	C
X	G	G	H	A	I	C	A	C	A

STRANGE	THORNY
TRUTH	PAIR
LUNGFISH	STRAW
COLONY	SLEEP
GRASS	GOSLING
ACACIA	HEAT
PREY	

Standards Link Language Arts: Spelling: Letter Sequencing; Reading: Vocabulary Development: Recognize Identical Words.

Kid Scoop ® | Health Tips

Which two bats are the same?

| Warning! | Germs on the ground! | Germs in the air! | Germs are everywhere! |

Clean Bats

We clean ourselves carefully every day, starting when we are very young.

Our wings must always stay moist so we lick them all over with a special fluid. The scent of this fluid makes it easier for mothers to find their young.

When our mothers go hunting, we hang together in "baby groups" to clean ourselves. We hang upside down from one foot and use the claw of the other foot as a comb.

Standards Links Science: Students Recognize that Animals Have Structures and Instincts that Serve Different Functions in Growth and Survival.

Belfry Bat's Good Health Tips

A long time ago, people thought bats were dirty creatures that spread disease. But actually, we are very clean animals and do a lot to help people!

The Vampire Cough

The way a movie vampire covers his face with his cape is a good way to stop the spread of germs. I call it the Vampire Cough. Next time you cough or sneeze, cough into the inside bend of your elbow. If you cough into your hand, the germs from your mouth will land on your hand and will get spread around. Think about it—what was the last thing you touched with the inside of your elbow!

Standards Link Health: Students Understand Behaviors that Prevent the Spread of Common Communicable Diseases and Learn Ways to Practice Good Hygiene.

Find the differences between these two vampires.

Standards Link Visual Discrimination: Students Find Similarities and Differences in Common Objects.

WHAT IS THE DIFFERENCE BETWEEN A BASEBALL PLAYER AND A VAMPIRE?

ANSWER: One bats flies: the other flies bats.

Name_____ Date _____

Pest Gobblers

Bats eat lots and lots of mosquitoes and other pesky insects. They are good to have around.

Can you "gobble" the germs? Look at these pictures of germs that make you sick. Seek them out on this page and destroy them!

Standards Link Health: Students Know Living Things Can Cause Beneficial Changes in the Environment.

Belfry Bat's Scare-Proof Halloween Promises

☑ I promise not to eat any treats until I come home and let an adult examine each one.

☑ I promise not to get into anyone's car unless I have permission from my parents.

☑ I promise not to go into anyone's house unless I have permission from my parents.

☑ I promise to listen to the person my parents have selected to take me out on Halloween night.

Standards Link Health: Students Recognize and Practice Safe Behaviors.

Clean Kids

Use Belfry Bat's secret code to find out how you can keep bad germs from getting you sick.

| A | D | E | H | I | N |
| O | P | R | S | T | W |

Standards Link Reading Comprehension: Follow Simple Written Directions.

Double Double Word Search

Find the words in the puzzle, then in the Kid Scoop stories and activities.

```
B S B E S E A R C H
L T E M Y R F L E B
F A R R O W B R Y G
B E A S I C K A E T
G R S N G P H R T O
O T G D H G M E A S
T S E P U S C A P E
L E M O H T H T V I
P S C L E A N M S G
```

BELFRY	CAPE
VAMPIRE	BATS
COUGH	COMB
GERMS	HOME
CLEAN	TREATS
WINGS	SICK

Standards Link Language Arts: Spelling: Letter Sequencing; Reading: Vocabulary Development: Recognize Identical Words.

BE A DINOSAUR DETECTIVE!

My name is Slate—**Sam Slate**. I'm a Dinosaur Detective, also known as a **paleontologist**.

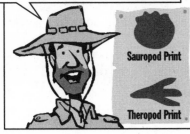

Sauropod Print

Theropod Print

In doing some research in this dry river bed, Sam discovered a group of dinosaur footprints. This is called a **trackway**. And trackways like this one are loaded with clues for Dinosaur Detectives!

Study the Trackway

These fossilized footprints tell Sam a lot about dinosaurs. They answer several mystery questions.

Help him separate out the footprints of the individual dinosaurs. Color all of the footprints with the number 1 the same color. Use another color for all the footprints with the number 2, and so on. The footprints of five different dinosaurs will appear.

Circle the answer to each dinosaur mystery question:

1. Which dinosaurs came to the riverbed first?

1   2   3   4   5

CLUE: Look to see which tracks have been stepped in. Top tracks came after bottom tracks.

2. Which dinosaurs were the biggest?

1   2   3   4   5

CLUE: Measure each dinosaur's stride. A stride is the distance between each step a dinosaur made. The footprints with larger strides came from larger dinosaurs.

3. Which dinosaur traveled with others of its kind?

Theropod   Sauropod

4. Which dinosaurs led the way?

Larger   Smaller

Theropods walked on two legs with a long, balancing tail.

Sauropods were large, four-footed, long-necked, plant eaters.

What do you call a dinosaur cowboy?

ANSWER: Tyrannosaurus Tex.

Name_____   Date _____

Dino Duos
Each dinosaur below has an identical twin. Find each matching pair.

Standards Link Scientific Investigation: Visual Discrimination: Find Similarities and Differences.

Name That Dinosaur

Circle the dinosaurs that are Sauropods.

Tyrannosaurus Rex

Triceratops

Stegosaurus

Sauropods were large, four-footed, long-necked plant-eaters.
Theropods walked on two legs with a long, balancing tail.

Standards Link Reading Comprehension: Students Demonstrate Comprehension by Identifying Answers in Text.

Double Double Word Search

Find the words in the puzzle, then in the Kid Scoop stories and activities.

S	K	C	A	R	T	D	D	D	R	E
D	T	E	S	C	S	E	U	L	C
O	T	I	G	T	C	A	F	O	V
P	Y	R	E	T	S	Y	M	P	S
O	E	E	L	O	W	O	F	L	T
R	D	V	N	I	D	I	G	A	A
U	F	I	C	T	I	O	N	N	I
A	D	R	N	O	S	A	U	T	L
S	T	N	I	R	P	T	O	O	F

DINOSAUR	TWIN
CLUES	MYSTERY
FOOTPRINTS	DUOS
SAUROPODS	LEGS
TRACKS	PLANT
RIVER	TAIL

Standards Link Language Arts: Spelling: Letter Sequencing; Reading: Vocabulary Development: Recognize Identical Words.

Kid Scoop — Children's Book Week

National Children's Book Week

Children's Book Week is always celebrated the week before Thanksgiving. It is a week to think about the books you love and to enjoy new books.

The first Book Week was celebrated in 1919. How many years ago was that?

Then, in 1921, a Book Week poster was designed to encourage children to read. A new poster has been designed every year since then.

Standards Link Math: Calculate Differences Using Dates.

Use the code to find out the slogan for the first Children's Book Week Poster.

⌐⌐ᗰ⌐ ⊙⌐⌐⊔⌐ ⋀⌐ ⌐⋖⌐ ⋖⌐⌐⌐

⊙	⌐	⋖	⋁	⊔	⌐	⌐	⌐	ᗰ	⌐	⌐
B	E	H	I	K	M	N	O	R	S	T

Standards Link Reading Comprehension: Follow Simple Directions.

Design a Poster

Imagine you could design a National Children's Book Week poster. What would your slogan be? What kind of picture would you put on your poster? Design your own Book Week poster.

Standards Link Reading Comprehension: Follow Simple Directions.

What if you couldn't read? If you couldn't read, the words on important signs might look like this. Learning to read is like finding a marvelous secret code. Use the decoder to find out what each sign says.

Standards Link Reading Comprehension: Follow Simple Directions.

στοπ
_ _ _ _

δανγερ!
_ _ _ _ _ _

ωετ παιντ
_ _ _ _ _ _ _ _

βεωαρε οφ δογ
_ _ _ _ _ _ _ _ _ _

δον'τ ωαλκ
_ _ _ _ _ _ _ _

πoισoν
_ _ _ _ _ _

SECRET DECODER

α = A	η = H	π = P
β = B	ι = I	ρ = R
δ = D	κ = K	σ = S
ε = E	λ = L	τ = T
φ = F	ν = N	ϖ = V
γ = G	o = O	ω = W

When is a green book not a green book?

ANSWER: When it is read (red).

Name_____ Date _____

START ▶

Help the bookworm find his way to the library.

END

Standards Link Physical Education: Eye Hand Coordination.

Picture Puzzle

Solve the puzzle to discover this year's National Children's Book Week slogan.

Standards Link Reading Comprehension: Follow Simple Directions.

Double Double
Word Search

Find the words in the puzzle, then in the Kid Scoop stories and activities.

E	N	A	R	R	K	N	I	H	T
R	T	I	O	E	N	J	O	Y	N
U	A	S	E	T	A	S	F	L	N
T	E	W	H	S	K	D	I	C	A
C	D	M	E	O	H	I	R	L	G
I	R	D	O	P	P	D	S	R	O
P	O	B	Y	H	E	P	T	N	L
C	W	U	N	G	I	S	E	D	S
S	B	B	L	I	B	R	A	R	Y

BOOKS   ENJOY

POSTER   SLOGAN

LIBRARY   PICTURE

READ   CODE

DESIGN   FIRST

WEEK   THINK

Standards Link Language Arts: Spelling: Letter Sequencing; Reading: Vocabulary Development: Recognize Identical Words.

Name_____ Date _____

Kid Scoop — Thanksgiving

Harvest of FUN!

Thanksgiving is the time to celebrate the harvest of grains, fruits, vegetables, and squashes. People celebrate with big feasts.

While the food is cooking, kids can have another kind of harvest —a harvest of fun and games!

Cornucopia of Words

Write the names of each food shown in the cornucopia on the lines below.

Standards Link Language Arts: Spelling: Matching Sounds to Letters.

_____
_____
_____
_____
_____
_____

Color!

Turkey Tail

Turkey wants to dress up for Thanksgiving. You can help. He wants his tail decorated with words that describe Thanksgiving.

But wait!

Turkey is particular about how the words are placed on his tail. They must be written onto the feathers from left to right in alphabetical order.

Standards Link Language Arts: Spelling: Alphabetize Vocabulary Words.

Find the Proverb

Look before you leap! Too many cooks spoil the broth! These are proverbs—sayings that give advice. One proverb is hidden in the leaf border. Start with the letter that is starred, and read every other letter as you go twice around the border.

Standards Link Language Arts: Spelling: Comprehend Basic Meanings of Proverbs; Follow Simple Written Directions.

What kind of **key** do you use on Thanksgiving?

A tur-key!

Name_____ Date _____

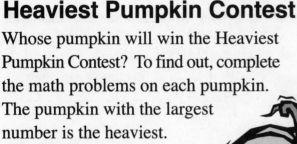

Heaviest Pumpkin Contest

Whose pumpkin will win the Heaviest
Pumpkin Contest? To find out, complete
the math problems on each pumpkin.
The pumpkin with the largest
number is the heaviest.

Standards Link Math: Number Sense: Solve
Addition and Subtraction Problems with One,
Two and Three Digits.

$$75 - 14$$

$$11 + 152$$

$$\begin{array}{r} 6 \\ 23 \\ +104 \end{array}$$

Moldy Harvest

Have you ever seen moldy stuff growing on old bread
or food in the fridge? There is one kind of mold that
has greatly improved people's chances of overcoming once-
dangerous illnesses. In 1928, a Scottish biologist, Alexander
Fleming, discovered a mold that could kill bacteria. This led
him to create the drug **penicillin**.

For many years after it was discovered, few people heard
about it because it could only be made in
very small amounts. Today penicillin
is widely used to treat ear
infections and other
illnesses and
infections.

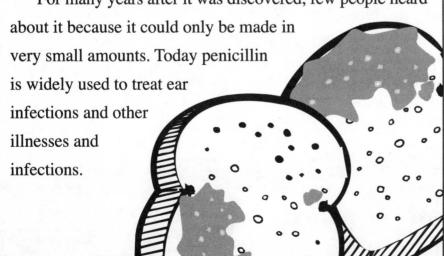

Standards Link Language Arts: Reading Comprehension. Science: Life Science: Some Changes in an Organism Are Beneficial.

Double Double Word Search

Find the words in the puzzle,
then in the Kid Scoop
stories and activities.

P	E	N	I	C	I	L	L	I	N
L	D	S	B	R	E	A	D	K	I
T	R	E	A	T	B	K	I	I	C
I	U	E	C	M	O	L	D	L	L
K	G	N	T	Y	S	M	A	L	L
I	N	F	E	C	T	I	O	N	S
N	F	B	R	L	U	Y	K	T	N
D	F	R	I	D	F	O	O	D	E
K	I	E	A	R	F	K	L	L	P

STUFF	EAR
BREAD	FOOD
MOLD	KIND
KILL	DRUG
BACTERIA	TREAT
SMALL	INFECTIONS
PENICILLIN	SEEN

Standards Link Language Arts: Spelling:
Letter Sequencing; Reading: Vocabulary
Development: Recognize Identical Words.

Name_____ Date _____

THE WRIGHT BROTHERS

Orville Wright flew the plane on the flight that made history. But it was the result of years of dreaming and designing by both Orville and his brother, Wilbur. The Wright brothers were bicycle makers from Dayton, Ohio, who loved to tinker and solve problems.

The big problem facing the Wright brothers and other pioneers of aviation was how to find a way of powering a craft. At time, the only choice was a steam engine, but it was too heavy for use in aircraft.

The invention of the lighter gasoline engine opened up the possibility of powered flight. In 1903, the Wright Flyer with its 12-horsepower engine made the dream of flight come true.

For years, the Wright brothers continued to come up with inventions that improved airplanes. Wilbur died in 1915. Before his death in 1948, Orville lived to see the airplane change the world. He saw the first regular airmail service, the first transcontinental flight in 1923, and the first round-the-world flight in 1924. He witnessed two world wars in which the airplane played an important role. He lived to see airplanes that traveled faster than the speed of sound.

Standards Link Genre: Reading Applications: Biography; Understanding Key People of an Historical Era; Identify How Some Things Change Over Time.

Cloud Maze

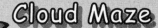

Help the pilot find the way through the clouds.

Standards Links Reading Comprehension; Physical Education: Eye Hand Coordination.

Start

Finish

Lift Happens

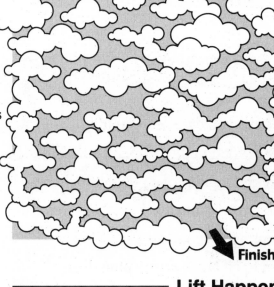

Hold a piece of paper between your fingers so that it hangs down in a curve. Blow as hard as you can across the top of the paper. What happens?

Standards Link Science Investigation: Follow a Set of Written Instructions for a Simple Investigation.

What was the greatest invention in the world?

KID SCOOP AIRLINES

ANSWER: The wheel, because it got everything rolling.

Name_____   Date _____

Flight Basics

Have you ever noticed that the wings of birds and planes are curved? Because of the curve, air rushing over the top of the wing has farther to go than under the wing, so it moves faster. Faster-moving air has a lower pressure, so the wing is lifted by the higher air pressure below.

A curved wing is called an **airfoil**.

Standards Link Science: Life Science; Recognize that Different Animals Have Different Features that Help Them Thrive.

Ducky Differences

Which duck is different from the rest?

Standards Link Science: Investigation: Observe Similarities and Differences in Objects; Follow Simple Directions.

First Powered Flight

From earliest times, people have dreamed of flying. Then, on December 17, 1903, Orville and Wilbur Wright made the dream come true with a 12-second wobbling flight of 120 feet over the sands of Kitty Hawk, North Carolina.

Before this historic date, several people around the world had managed to take flight in gliders, which were really no more than huge kites. The Wright brothers' feat was important because it was the first engine-powered flight, and would eventually lead to other kinds of flight that are common today.

Standards Link Reading Applications: Genre: Biography.

Double Double Word Search

Find the words in the puzzle, then in the Kid Scoop stories and activities.

W	H	A	W	K	K	I	T	T	Y
R	O	M	Z	Y	E	U	R	T	M
I	D	R	U	B	L	I	W	T	K
G	S	N	L	C	L	K	F	O	I
H	S	R	E	D	I	L	G	S	T
T	N	Y	R	A	V	T	H	A	E
S	L	E	T	R	R	E	U	N	S
D	A	T	E	U	O	E	G	D	W
M	T	H	G	I	L	F	E	S	C

WORLD   WRIGHT
HUGE   DATE
WILBUR   HAWK
FLIGHT   DREAM
KITES   GLIDERS
KITTY   TRUE
SANDS   ORVILLE

Standards Link Language Arts: Spelling: Letter Sequencing; Reading: Vocabulary Development: Recognize Identical Words.

The Story of Christmas Seals

One stormy December night in 1903, a mail carrier named Elinar Holboell was working late in a small post office just outside of Copenhagen, Denmark.

Glancing out the window, he noticed two children dressed in rags. As he went back to his work sorting the happy holiday cards, he was troubled by the hungry and cold children.

Suddenly he had an idea. Suppose that every letter carried an extra stamp, and the money from these stamps helped unfortunate children.

In 1904, Elinar and his fellow postal workers created a special stamp to help children. It had a picture of the queen of Denmark, Queen Louise.

The Danes bought four million seals that first year. The funds were used to build hospitals for children with tuberculosis (TB). At that time, TB was the leading cause of death.

How Christmas Seals Came to America
Denmark's neighbors, Norway and Sweden, saw what a great power the people could be, and in 1905 they started selling Christmas Seals.

But when an American woman wanted to use Christmas Seals to save a small hospital in Pennsylvania, she ran into problems. The post office would not let its workers sell the seals.

When a young newspaper writer saw the seals, he told his boss, "Just look—a penny apiece—within everyone's reach—think how they'll carry the news of what people can do for themselves—what a slogan, *STAMP OUT TUBERCULOSIS!*"

The newspaper told the story and sold the seals at their front counter. The first day the stamps went on sale, a little newsboy who was too small to see over the counter came in and, reaching up with a penny, said, "Gimme one. Me sister's got it."

Stamp Out Tuberculosis
Soon, countries around the world started selling Christmas Seals to help people with TB. Today, TB is not the threat that it was 60 years ago. But there is still a need for help. Today the money from the sale of Christmas Seals helps people with asthma, bronchitis, and other diseases of the lungs.

Help Elinar sort the mail.
Draw a line from each envelope to the box it should go in. Unscramble the names of the cities on the map. Then draw a line from each box of mail to that city's location on the map.

Standards Link Reading Comprehension: Follow Multiple-step Directions.

Standards Link History: Students Understand How Events in the Present Are Connected to the Past and the Importance of Civic Virtue.

Why did the boy jump up and down on the letter?

ANSWER: He heard that you have to stamp letters or the post office won't send them.

Name_____ Date _____

Find the hidden pictures.

Standards Link Science: Investigation and Observation.

Find the stamp that is different.

Standards Link Scientific Investigation: Identifying Similarities and Differences in Common Objects.

Which stamp comes next?

Look for a pattern in each row of stamps. Draw the stamp that comes next.

Standards Link Math: Students Recognize Patterns.

Double Double Word Search

Find the words in the puzzle, then in the Kid Scoop stories and activities.

P	A	M	D	Y	M	R	O	T	S
M	G	F	W	O	R	K	E	R	S
P	M	A	T	S	G	N	U	L	Y
N	E	W	S	P	A	P	E	R	A
E	O	R	A	N	E	E	U	Q	D
D	P	R	A	G	S	N	L	U	I
E	N	T	W	S	L	N	I	E	L
W	N	K	H	A	D	Y	A	T	O
S	E	A	L	S	Y	V	M	P	H

STAMP	RAGS
PENNY	HOLIDAY
SEALS	WORKERS
SWEDEN	LUNGS
NEWSPAPER	QUEEN
NORWAY	MAIL
STORMY	MAP

Standards Link Language Arts: Spelling: Letter Sequencing; Reading: Vocabulary Development: Recognize Identical Words.

Name_____ Date _____

2000
1999
1998

How Old Is Your Christmas Tree?

Each year, a tree grows a new layer of wood under its bark. By counting these layers, called rings, you can discover the age of a tree.

This year, after you take the decorations off your Christmas tree, count its rings! One ring equals one year. (The bark is not a ring.) Can you find out the age of your tree?

Here's the trunk of my Christmas tree.

> My name is Dr. Cypress Sapling. I'm a dendrochronologist. What's that? Well, a dendrochronologist is a scientist who studies the rings of trees.

The rings of a tree can also show what the climate of the forest was during different years. Look at the tree trunk pictured above. Some of the rings are wide and some of them are thin. A wide ring tells us that this was a good year for growing. There was the right amount of water and sunlight. Drought causes slower growth and narrow rings. Dark spots tell us that the tree survived a fire that year.

Reading Rings Tells Past

By reading the rings of trees, dendrochronologists can read the story of our planet, stories that reside in living trees and in logs used to build ancient buildings. Tree rings have told of weather patterns that lead to severe fires. They have revealed century-long droughts, insect plagues, and times of volcanic eruptions.

Standards Link Science: When the Environment Changes, Plant Growth and Survival Are Affected.

> My Christmas tree survived a fire one year. What year was that? In what year was my tree planted? Is my tree older than you? Find the ring that grew in 1997. Was this a good growing year for the tree?

ORNAMENTS

Standards Link Math: Students Use Strategies, Skills, and Concepts in Finding Solutions.

What did the tree say to the beaver?

ANSWER: "Leaf me alone!"

Name_____ Date_____

Kid Scoop — Tree Rings

Read the Rings

Core sample from living tree

I don't have to cut down trees to read their rings. Using a special tool called an *increment borer*, I can take a core sample from a living tree. A core sample is about the size of a soda straw, and the rings look like lines.

I found an old log cabin while hiking last week. I took a core sample from the logs to find the age of the cabin.

Core sample from Christmas tree

Core sample from log cabin

Compare the core samples to see where the patterns of the rings match. The last ring of the living tree grew in the year 2000. Count backwards from the bark to find out the age of each tree. Cutting out the strips makes comparing easier.

Use the core samples to complete the chart below.

	Age of the tree	Year tree was cut down	Year tree was planted
LIVING TREE			
DR. SAPLING'S CHRISTMAS TREE			
LOG FROM CABIN			

Standards Link Math: Use a Table to Sort Information and Compute Results.

Tree Ring Maze

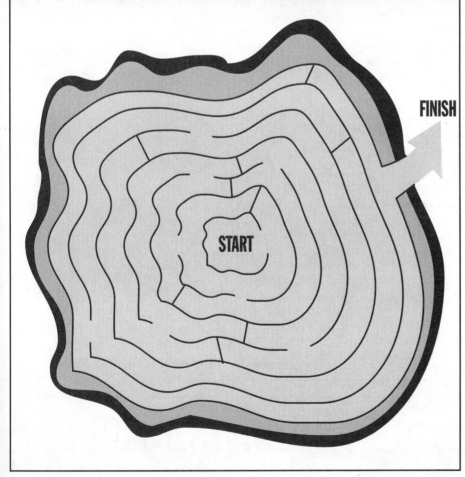

FINISH

START

Standards Link Physical Education: Eye Hand Coordination.

Double Double Word Search

Find the words in the puzzle, then in the Kid Scoop stories and activities.

D	R	E	H	T	A	E	W	N	P
E	N	D	R	E	R	O	C	I	R
O	S	G	T	G	C	H	O	B	E
R	E	K	R	A	B	S	U	A	D
O	L	N	E	O	N	G	N	C	I
O	P	U	E	L	W	N	T	F	C
O	M	R	S	O	G	I	I	I	T
S	A	T	O	B	A	R	N	T	S
R	S	D	E	A	E	D	G	G	R

GROWING   FIRE
TREES   CORE
RINGS   CABIN
WOOD   AGE
BARK   SAMPLES
COUNTING   WEATHER
TRUNK

Standards Link Language Arts: Spelling: Letter Sequencing; Reading: Vocabulary Development: Recognize Identical Words.

Name_____ Date_____

RAINBOW POWER

Rainbows are beautiful to look at because they are made of many different colors. They have the power to make us feel happy, just by looking at them.

Martin Luther King Jr. saw that there were many different colors of people in the world. He believed that these differences could make the world a better place to live. He spent his life helping people live together in peace and equality.

Today we celebrate Martin Luther King's birthday because of his great work and his important message: that all people are precious and that our differences, like a rainbow, can make the world a better place.

Standards Link History: Students Identify the People Honored in Commemorative Holidays, Including the Human Struggles that Were the Basis for the Events.

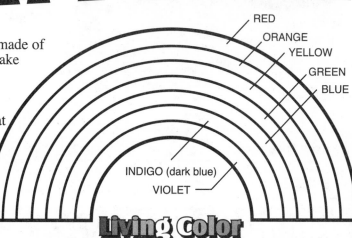

RED
ORANGE
YELLOW
GREEN
BLUE
INDIGO (dark blue)
VIOLET

Living Color

Color the one above with the real colors of a rainbow. Color each child in the rainbow below a different color of people.

"Our flag is red, white, and blue, but our nation is a rainbow— red, yellow, brown, black, and white."
– Jesse Jackson

E P
C
A E

What's at the end of the rainbow?

What could be at the end of a rainbow of people? A pot of gold—or something better? Unscramble the letters on the coins to spell something you might find if all people appreciated each others' differences.

_ _ _ _ _

Standards Link Social Science: Students Recognize the Forms of Diversity in Their Community and the Benefits of a Diverse Population.

What is red, white, blue, and yellow?

ANSWER: A star-spangled banana.

Kid Scoop — Martin Luther King Jr.

Together at Last

Do some research and find an article and/or picture that shows people of different races working together. Glue the picture or the article in the first box.

In the second box, write what you think Martin Luther King Jr. would have said about these people.

Standards Link Social Science: Students Recognize the Ways in which They Are All Part of the Same Community, Sharing Principles, Goals, and Traditions Despite Their Varied Ancestry; Understand Ways in which Groups Interact with One Another to Try to Resolve Problems.

Friendship Maze

Help the rainbow friends meet at the center of the maze.

Standards Links Reading Comprehension: Follow Simple Written Instructions.

Double Double Word Search

Find the words in the puzzle, then in the Kid Scoop stories and activities.

R	G	N	I	P	L	E	H	S	A
I	N	W	O	B	N	I	A	R	P
M	N	A	T	I	O	N	R	O	E
E	A	B	J	E	S	S	E	L	O
C	O	R	C	G	W	E	H	O	P
A	P	A	T	N	V	O	T	C	L
L	E	Y	T	I	L	A	U	Q	E
P	W	E	L	K	N	D	L	O	G
R	A	R	E	H	T	E	G	O	T

RAINBOW   NATION
PEACE   PEOPLE
EQUALITY   HELPING
MARTIN   TOGETHER
LUTHER   LIVE
KING   PLACE
COLORS   JESSE
GOLD

Standards Link Language Arts: Spelling: Letter Sequencing; Reading: Vocabulary Development: Recognize Identical Words.

Kid Scoop

Weather

DR. I. CICLE'S WEATHER SCHOOL

I'm puzzled, Dr. Cicle. What are cold fronts and warm fronts?

Good question, Paula! Cold fronts and warm fronts are something meteorologists— scientists who study the weather—watch to make predictions about the weather.

Here's how meteorologists show a cold front on a map.

This is how they show a warm front.

The cold front looks like icicles on a string!

Standards Link Science: Students Understand How to Read a Weather Map.

Oh no! A cold wind blew my display about weather fronts all apart! Luckily, I numbered each sentence. Do the math problem on each piece. Then use the answers to put the sentences in order from the smallest number to the largest.

8+7=
Cold fronts move quickly and can bring storms and even hail. But the storms won't last long.

4+3=
The sun's heat warms the air. Some parts of the world get warmer than others. These differences in temperature make the air move, causing weather to change.

20-8=
This cools the warm air, and if there is moisture in that air, it condenses and forms drops that fall as rain or snow.

19-3=
A "warm front" moves slowly. If the air is moist, dark clouds will form and it may rain or snow for days.

6+3=
A "cold front" happens when a cold air mass pushes the warm air up.

17-9=
When cold and warm air masses meet, they don't mix. They form a front.

Standards Link Math: Students Compute Sums and Differences, Order Numbers from Least to Greatest.

What song do you sing at a snowman's birthday party?

ANSWER: Freeze a Jolly Good Fellow.

Independent Activity Pages for Reading

Scholastic

Name_____ Date _____

Help Paula Predict the Weather

Look at the two weather puzzles. Which town is most likely to have stormy weather? Use the cold front and warm front symbols to help you predict.

Standards Link Science: Students Understand that Weather Can be Observed and Predicted; Different Conditions Affect Different Results.

Snowman Match Game

Chill out while you find the two identical snowmen.

Standards Link Scientific Investigation: Identifying Similarities and Differences in Common Objects.

Double Double Word Search

Find the words in the puzzle, then in the Kid Scoop stories and activities.

E	R	U	T	S	I	O	M	S	P
S	N	O	S	D	C	F	R	E	R
T	L	A	L	M	O	R	F	S	E
O	M	O	R	L	E	O	G	N	D
R	C	A	B	H	D	N	W	E	I
M	W	T	T	M	O	T	A	D	C
S	P	A	M	L	Y	S	T	N	T
N	E	M	W	O	N	S	C	O	N
W	T	S	A	L	L	I	H	C	S

WEATHER	MOISTURE
FRONTS	CHILL
SYMBOLS	COLD
CONDENSES	MASS
STORMS	LAST
SNOWMEN	LONG
WARM	PREDICT
WATCH	

Standards Link Language Arts: Spelling: Letter Sequencing; Reading: Vocabulary Development: Recognize Identical Words.

Name_____ Date _____

The Power of the Pen

A Horrible Crime

Ida B. Wells

Imagine how you would feel if three of your friends were mobbed and killed.

On March 8, 1892, three white men broke into a grocery store in Memphis, Tennessee. The three black owners fired at the robbers. But when the police arrived, they arrested the store owners and put them in jail.

At about 2 a.m. the next morning, an angry mob hustled the store owners out of jail and brutally shot them to death.

A Force for Change

Ida B. Wells knew the murdered men. In those days, "lynchings," or murders by angry mobs, were common in the South. For the most part the mobs were white and the victims were black.

As the editor and part owner of the *Memphis Free Speech* newspaper, Wells wrote an article protesting these killings. Three months later, while on a trip to New York City, she learned that her newspaper offices had been wrecked and her life was threatened. She couldn't go back to Memphis.

Wells found a job with a black newspaper in New York. For the rest of her life, she continued to fight for the rights of people to live without fear of being lynched. Many changes occurred because of her courageous use of the power of the pen.

Although her story was not found in most history books until very recently, the United States Postal Service issued a stamp in 1990 honoring Ida B. Wells.

Source: *Ida B. Wells-Barnett and the Antilynching Crusade* by Suzanne Freedman

Standards Link History: Students Understand the Problems of the Past and the Contributions of Many Cultures to Our American Ideals.

Read the story and number the pictures so that they are in the correct order.

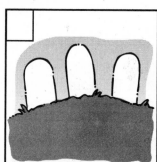

Standards Link Reading Comprehension: Sequencing Events.

What is the tallest building in Tennessee?

Answer: The library. It has the most stories.

What would you say?

Imagine you are Ida B. Wells. Write an article about what you think of lynching.

On the top line, write a headline for your article. Then write your name.

Use the lines to write your article.

By _____

Standards Link Writing Applications: Writing Using Newspaper Format in a Content Area.

PUZZLING PENS

Can you find the pens in the square below that are in the same order as the ones at left? Look up, down, and across.

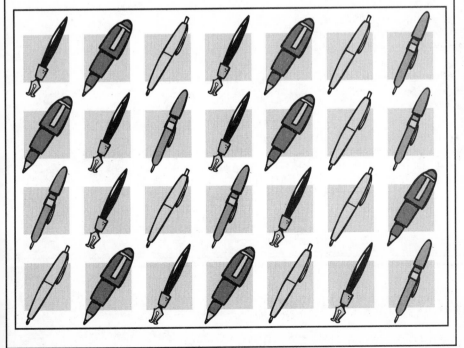

Standards Link Science: Investigation and Observation.

Double Double Word Search

Find the words in the puzzle, then in the Kid Scoop stories and activities.

P	O	W	E	R	L	D	L	I	L
L	G	R	O	C	E	R	Y	D	E
A	N	E	W	Y	R	G	N	A	T
R	C	C	W	R	O	P	C	O	T
T	Y	K	P	O	B	W	H	R	E
I	M	E	N	T	B	G	E	D	R
C	D	D	C	S	E	R	D	E	S
L	G	R	O	T	R	I	P	R	Q
E	R	A	U	Q	S	L	L	E	W

NEW POWER
IDA SQUARE
GROCERY ARTICLE
ANGRY STORY
ROBBERS ORDER
TRIP MEN
WRECKED WELLS
LYNCHED

Standards Link Language Arts: Spelling: Letter Sequencing; Reading: Vocabulary Development: Recognize Identical Words.

Name_____ Date _____

YOUR TREASURE CHEST

You have a treasure chest with you every day. Inside your chest there is a treasure that keeps you alive. It is your heart.

Your heart is in the middle of your chest, a little to the left. Put your hand on your chest and be very still. Can you feel your heart beating?

Your heart is actually a muscle, a very strong muscle.

It pumps blood to all parts of your body. It works all the time, even when you're sleeping.

Think about how you would make other muscles in your body strong, such as your arm or leg muscles. Exercise, followed by rest and good eating habits, is the key to a strong muscle and a healthy treasure chest.

Standards Link Health: Make Decisions About Food, Rest, Exercise and Hygiene, which Maintain and Enhance Health.

Can you find the keys to strong muscles and a healthy treasure chest?

Peek inside your treasure chest!

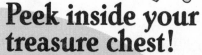

Arteries

Real hearts don't look much like valentine hearts. Inside the treasure chest is a picture of a real heart. The tubes that stick out from the heart are the arteries and veins that carry blood to and from all parts of your body. Arteries carry your blood from the heart to your body, to deliver oxygen. Veins carry the blood, minus oxygen, back to your heart.

To find out the size of your heart, make a fist with one hand. This is about the size of your heart.

Standards Link Science: Animals Have Structures that Serve Different Functions In Growth and Survival.

Veins

Jumping Jewel

Your heart needs exercise, just like all of the other muscles in your body. The faster you move, the faster your heart beats. Beating faster for a while every day is good exercise for a heart.

Place two fingers on the inner side of your left wrist. Do you feel a little jump? This is the blood from your heart going to your hand. You can feel that jump every time your heart beats. This is called your **pulse**.

Jump up and down 10 times. Is your pulse faster or slower?

Standards Link Health: Understand the Importance of Regular Exercise to Maintain and Enhance Health.

Have Cupid's eyes ever been checked?

 ANSWER: No, they've always been plain blue.

Kid Scoop Healthy Hearts

Heart Smart Treasure Puzzle

Discover the hidden treasure!

To find it, read each list of foods at right and pick the one that is lowest in saturated fat. Then color the letter of that choice on the grid and discover the hidden treasure!

Heart Smart Clue

Foods high in saturated fat add cholesterol to your blood. Too much cholesterol can be bad for your heart. It can cause the arteries that bring blood to your heart to clog up.

Standards Link Scientific Investigation: Find Similarities and Differences in Common Objects.

K	X	F	P	B
I	O		L	D
C	E	J	V	U
S	R	A	H	G
W	M	N	Q	T

1. **W:** whole milk, **N:** skim milk, **G:** low-fat milk
2. **P:** baked fish, **Q:** fried chicken
3. **E:** muffin, **S:** doughnut, **R:** bagel
4. **U:** 2 tsp. of margarine, **K:** 2 tsp. of butter, **A:** 2 tsp. of cream cheese
5. **X:** baked potato, **B:** French fries
6. **O:** a slice of pepperoni pizza, **D:** a slice of cheese pizza
7. **T:** quarter-pound cheeseburger, **I:** plain roast beef (3 oz) sandwich, **J:** fried fish sandwich
8. **F:** mayonnaise, **C:** mustard, **V:** low-calorie mayonnaise
9. **L:** ice cream, **M:** apple pie, **H:** low-fat frozen yogurt

PULSE PUZZLE

Which animal has the fastest heart rate? To find out, draw a line to match the heart parts. The number inside the matched parts tells how many times that animal's heart beats in one minute.

Standards Link Science: Heart Rate Is Related to Size in Animals.

Double Double Word Search

Find the words in the puzzle, then in the Kid Scoop stories and activities.

A	M	E	F	P	S	T	A	E	B
R	U	I	P	E	E	K	V	X	E
E	S	R	V	R	P	N	O	E	G
T	C	I	T	U	T	I	T	R	N
S	L	A	M	S	N	R	U	C	O
A	E	P	E	A	A	I	B	I	R
F	S	H	K	E	Y	S	E	S	T
M	C	A	H	R	X	E	S	E	S
W	R	I	S	T	D	O	O	L	B

TREASURE	PUMPS
HEART	CHEST
EXERCISE	STRONG
BLOOD	TUBES
ALIVE	WRIST
KEYS	FASTER
BEATS	PEEK
MUSCLES	

Standards Link Language Arts: Spelling: Letter Sequencing; Reading: Vocabulary Development: Recognize Identical Words.

Thank you from the bottom of our hearts!

Thank you to the American Heart Association for their help with this page. More educational information and teacher resources are available at their web site.
www.americanheart.org/Health/Lifestyle/Youth/heartpower/

Name_____ Date _____

Mammoth Ice Cube

Tusk Trip

One day, a man was out hunting in Siberia, when suddenly he tripped!

Looking down, he saw that he had tripped over a tusk! A mammoth tusk!

Scientists came to study the tusk and found that it was attached to an entire frozen prehistoric mammoth. Trying to dig up the mammoth proved difficult. The frozen ground, or permafrost, was as hard as cement!

Read the scientists' notebook to see how to get a mammoth out of the ground. Number the pictures in the correct order.

Standards Link Reading Comprehension: Identify the Elements of a Story by Retelling the Order in which They Occurred.

How to get a mammoth out of the frozen ground.

1. Use a jackhammer to dig a trench around the mammoth.

2. Drill holes under the mammoth.

3. Insert steel poles through the holes.

4. Connect the steel poles to strong cable and hook this to a helicopter.

5. Lift the mammoth out of the ground.

Help the helicopter get to the cave.

In October 1999, the 24-ton block of ice with the mammoth's body inside was taken by helicopter to a frozen cave some 200 miles away in Khatanga.

Standards Link Physical Education: Eye Hand Coordination.

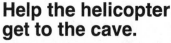

When will a net hold water?

ANSWER: When the water is frozen into ice.

Name_____ Date _____

Mammoth Math

Do the math to find out some extraordinary facts about the woolly mammoth.

Mammoths were the largest land mammals that ever existed. They lived throughout the Northern Hemisphere for about
85,000 + 15,000 =
_____ years.

The word "mammoth" is used to describe something incredibly large—and that is what these animals were. They weighed around
9 - 2 =
_____ tons.

From the size of its molars, scientists determined that the frozen mammoth was
(5 x 9) + 2=
_____ years old when it died.

It took more than a year to thaw the mammoth using
5 + 7=
_____ hair dryers.

Standards Link Math: Compute Sums Using +, -, x, and Order of Operations.

STINKY BUT TRUE!

Dick Mol, one of the scientists studying the mammoth, discovered that science can be smelly. While helping thaw the frozen mammoth, he noticed that it smelled like the elephant exhibit at the zoo!

Melting Mix-up

The scientists thawed the mammoth very slowly and used a sieve to filter out all ancient insects and plant material that was stuck in the mammoth's fur.

Can you find eight silly things hiding in this mammoth's fur?

Standards Link Scientific Investigation: Identifying Common Objects.

Double Double Word Search

Find the words in the puzzle, then in the Kid Scoop stories and activities.

```
N S T U C K F F T R
E L E E T S O O N M
Z D A E R U H S E T
O H D E R T F E M T
R E T P O C I L E H
F R R M O A Z O C A
E U M N N V O P R W
F A S I B E R I A E
M S T C E S N I T D
```

MAMMOTH	CEMENT
CAVE	STEEL
SIBERIA	POLES
FROZEN	INSECTS
THAWED	FUR
HELICOPTER	READ
TUSK	

Standards Link Language Arts: Spelling: Letter Sequencing; Reading: Vocabulary Development: Recognize Identical Words.

Name_____ Date _____

The Race Is On!

The race began on March 3, 2001. Mushers and their sled dogs sped off into the arctic wilderness, all competing to come in first in the race known as the Iditarod.

Remember the "Race Against Death"

About one hundred years ago, gold was discovered in Alaska. The Iditarod Trail connected mining towns and camps from Anchorage to Nome. The trail was named after the town of Iditarod, which some say means a far distant place. Teams of dogs pulled sleds with mail and supplies to the miners and then returned to Anchorage loaded with gold.

After the gold rush, the trail was seldom used.

In the winter of 1925, an epidemic of a deadly disease, diphtheria, broke out in Nome. The closest medicine was in Anchorage. Twenty sled-dog mushers and their dogs battled the weather and arctic wilderness to get the life-saving medicine to Nome.

To bring recognition to this historic trail, the Iditarod Trail Sled Dog Race was started in 1973.

Standards Link History: Students Understand Key Events of a Historical Era and Explain How the Present Is Connected to the Past.

Where Did They Go?

Three teams of dogs and their mushers set out across the arctic wilderness. Follow the directions for each team. Write where they end up on the line.

BLUE TEAM

1. Start in Seward.
2. Travel 3 spaces north.
3. Travel 2 spaces west.
4. Travel 3 spaces north.
5. Travel 2 spaces west.
6. Travel 1 space south.
7. Travel 2 spaces west.

_____

Map showing ALASKA with Yukon River, Nome, Fairbanks, Nenana, Iditarod, Kuskokwim River, Anchorage, Seward. Compass: N, W, E, S.

RED TEAM

1. Start in Fairbanks.
2. Travel 2 spaces north.
3. Travel 3 spaces west.
4. Travel 4 spaces south.
5. Travel 1 space west.
6. Travel 1 space south.

_____

YELLOW TEAM

1. Start in Anchorage.
2. Travel 4 spaces west.
3. Travel 3 spaces north.
4. Travel 6 spaces east.
5. Travel 1 space north.
6. Travel 2 spaces west.

_____

Standards Link Reading Comprehension: Students Follow Simple Written Directions.

What do you call a hot pepper at the North Pole?

ANSWER: A chilly chili.

Name_____ Date _____

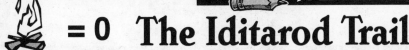
The Iditarod Trail

Use the code at left to find out about the actual Iditarod Trail.

 = 0
 = 1
(snowflake) = 2
(sled) = 3
(tree) = 4
(paw) = 9

The trail is  miles long. The trail crosses over ❄ mountain ranges and takes  from 🐾 to ❄🦴 days, depending on the weather.

Standards Link Reading Comprehension: Students Follow Simple Multiple-step Directions.

Web Search

The Internet has a blizzard of resources on the Iditarod. You can follow the race and even write a report on its history, geography, mushers, and more!

Some say that racing dogs across the frigid arctic is cruel. Different web sites discuss this important topic. Do your research and then write a paragraph telling what you think.

Standards Link Research/Technology; Students Locate Electronic Information. Writing; Establish a Main Idea and Develop the Topic with Simple Facts, Details, Examples and Explanations.

Husky Heroes

"The dogs are the real champions."
– *Susan Butcher*, *four-time winner of the Iditarod*

Which two huskies are exactly alike?

Standards Link Scientific Investigation: Students Recognize Similarities and Differences in Common Objects.

Double Double Word Search

Find the words in the puzzle, then in the Kid Scoop stories and activities.

I	D	D	I	G	I	R	F	D	D
I	T	S	G	O	D	S	O	R	L
A	R	M	I	N	E	R	S	A	O
A	K	S	A	L	A	E	L	Z	G
E	M	O	N	T	R	H	E	Z	H
C	O	D	I	T	C	S	D	I	U
A	R	D	A	I	T	U	S	L	S
R	I	A	R	T	I	M	L	B	K
S	S	P	M	A	C	L	E	D	Y

IDITAROD   MUSHERS
HUSKY   RACE
BLIZZARD   ALASKA
ARCTIC   CAMPS
NOME   DOGS
MINERS   GOLD
SLEDS   FRIGID

Standards Link Language Arts: Spelling: Letter Sequencing; Reading: Vocabulary Development: Recognize Identical Words.

Money

Leprechaun's Green Trivia

Read Leprechaun's trivia about the color green, and then help him collect his golden coins on his way to his pot o' gold.

Standards Link Visual Discrimination.

Can you find the four-leaf clover?

Worn-out Greens

When is a dollar bill worth nothing at all? When there is less than half of a bill, or if it is too old and worn to be used, it has no value.

Old, worn, and torn bills are collected by banks. They send them to a government office that shreds the bills into tiny pieces. Each year billions of these shredded dollars end up in dumps!

Standards Link Social Science: Children Understand Basic Economic Concepts.

Why is U.S. money green?

The ink used to make U.S. dollars is made from a secret mix of green and black ink that is very difficult to match. This makes it hard for anyone except the government to make money.

Standards Link Social Science: Children Understand Basic Economic Concepts.

A cow for your thoughts?

Before coins were invented, people traded things —like cows for seeds, or tools for chickens.

People started using metal coins about 2,000 years ago, and many of the first coins were shaped like cows!

Coins soon became popular. After all, they were a lot easier to carry around than cows!

Standards Link Social Science: Children Understand Basic Economic Concepts.

Hmmph!

TODAY'S SPECIAL - 30 CHICKENS FOR 1 COW

Wrapped in Greenbacks

The U.S. government sells some very special wrapping paper. It is whole sheets of real money! Each sheet is made up of dollar bills that have not been cut apart.

If someone gives you a gift wrapped in money, you can cut out and spend each of the dollar bills.

Standards Link Social Science: Children Understand Basic Economic Concepts.

Pot O' Gold

What gives milk, goes "moo, moo," and makes all your dreams come true?

ANSWER: Your Dairy Godmother.

Name_____ Date _____

Where's Betty's Bovine?

Betty brought her **bovine** (another word for cow) to market and she has disappeared. Can you help Betty find her?

LOST COW!

My cow has some big spots, and some small ones. She was not wearing a bell. She has horns, but not sharp ones. She has a clump of dark hair on her head. Her tail is not short.

Betty

Standards Link Scientific Investigation: Identify Similarities and Differences in Common Objects.

Crunchy Cash

Imagine what it would be like to go shopping if we paid for things with crunchy food. Let's say that different foods are worth the following:

1 peanut = 1¢   **1 carrot = 25¢**

1 apple = 10¢   **1 cookie = 5¢**

1 bag of chips = $1

Chomp on this challenge!

Carlos bought two comic books, a set of markers, and an ice cream sundae. How much "crunchy cash" did he spend?

Kid Scoop Shop

COMICS $4.19   35¢ $1.45   98¢

Standards Link Math: Solve Problems Involving Money Amounts; Follow Multiple-step Processes.

Double Double Word Search

Find the words in the puzzle, then in the Kid Scoop stories and activities.

S	D	A	C	O	V	M	R	S	P
B	W	R	A	P	P	I	N	G	M
O	C	O	S	T	D	I	E	B	A
V	A	G	C	M	O	N	E	Y	R
I	S	R	E	C	L	T	P	L	K
N	H	T	O	O	L	S	A	L	E
E	A	C	H	M	A	W	P	A	T
L	O	O	V	G	R	E	E	N	N
T	S	E	E	D	S	S	R	H	E

COINS   SEEDS
DOLLARS   METAL
GREEN   TOOLS
MONEY   BOVINE
WRAPPING   CASH
PAPER   EACH
COWS   MARKET

Standards Link Language Arts: Spelling: Letter Sequencing; Reading: Vocabulary Development: Recognize Identical Words.

Name_____ Date_____

Kid Scoop — Amelia Earhart

THE ADVENTURE OF FLIGHT

Long before there were airplanes, people dreamed of flying. Courageous dreamers like the Wright brothers made the dream a reality.

The first pilots were always testing the limits of speed, distance, and altitude.

One pilot also challenged the role of women. Her name was Amelia Earhart.

When Amelia was a young woman, it was not considered "ladylike" to become a pilot. Very few women had ever learned to fly. But Amelia was raised to be her own person and to follow her heart.

In 1920, she paid $1 for a 10-minute ride in an airplane. "As soon as I left the ground," she wrote later, "I knew I myself had to fly." Little did she know that she would become one of the world's most famous pilots.

Standards Link Reading Comprehension: Genre: Biography.

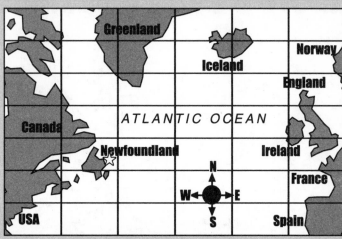

Transatlantic Trip

Amelia Earhart set many flying records. As a crew member of the Friendship Flight in 1928, she was the first woman ever to fly across the Atlantic.

Four years later, Amelia flew her own plane across the vast Atlantic Ocean alone.

Where did she land? Follow these instructions and use the map to find out.

Take off from Newfoundland. Travel two spaces east. Move one space north. Fly east two spaces and land safely on the island in the lower left side of that space. Where are you?

Standards Link Geography: Students Students Use Map Skills to Determine Location.

Help this plane find its way through the stormy sky.

A Capitol Idea

Amelia Earhart and First Lady Eleanor Roosevelt once left a dinner party and took a night flight above Washington, D.C. —in their evening gowns!

What eight-letter word starts with g-a-s?

ANSWER: Airplane.

Name_____ Date _____

The Earhart Mystery

Amelia wanted to be the first person to fly around the world. In 1937, she took off from Oakland, California.

Near the end of her journey, all contact was lost and Amelia Earhart was never heard from again. Some say she crashed. Others think she landed on a South Pacific island and stayed there the rest of her life.

The story of her disappearance remains a mystery. But it is the story of her life that inspires others to great courage. She blazed new trails in flying, shaping advancements in flight that we enjoy today.

Standards Link History/Social Science: Students Understand the Contributions of Famous Americans.

Find a word that rhymes with each of these airplane parts:

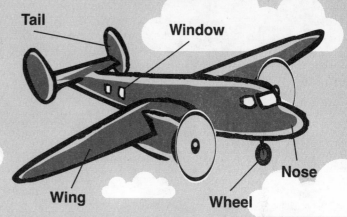

Tail
Window
Nose
Wheel
Wing

Standards Link Language Arts: Phonemic Awareness; Recognize and Produce Rhyming Words.

Crazy Cockpit

Find eight silly things that don't belong in this airplane's cockpit.

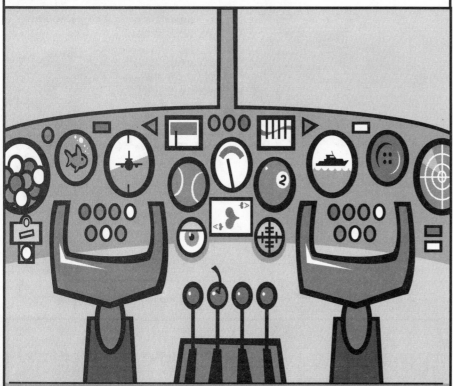

Standards Link Scientific Investigation: Classifying Objects by Common Characteristics.

Double Double Word Search

Find the words in the puzzle, then in the Kid Scoop stories and activities.

```
T O L I P D Y M I C
F R I Z W E R C Y I
P L A N E E K N L T
F S T H I P O G F N
L R N T R S M Y L A
Y A D E Z A L B Y L
I E N U W R E A I T
N Y A L O N E T N A
G F L I G H T K T D
```

ATLANTIC   SPEED
CREW   TAIL
PILOT   LAND
EARHART   FLYING
BLAZED   ALONE
PLANE   FLIGHT
ISLAND   YEARS

Standards Link Language Arts: Spelling: Letter Sequencing; Reading: Vocabulary Development: Recognize Identical Words.

Name_____ Date _____

You're a GEM!

You know you have a birthDAY. Did you know you also have a birthSTONE? A special gemstone has been selected to be the birthstone for each month of the year.

Discover Your Birthstone

1. Find the month you were born in the list below.

2. Next to your birthday month, there are two symbols. The first symbol shows you which horizontal line to follow on the Intergalactic Gemstone Locator Grid. The second symbol tells you which vertical line to follow.

3. The gem at the point where the two lines meet is your personal birthstone!

Standards Link: Math: Measure Time Using Calendars. Reading Comprehension: Follow Simple Written Directions.

▼8 January
C▲ February
=O March
C■ April
★II May
=■ June
★O July
-●-▲ August
▼II September
-●-■ October
=▲ November
-●-O December

INTERGALACTIC GEMSTONE LOCATOR GRID

Topaz
Pearl
Aquamarine
Sapphire
Amethyst
Garnet
Emerald
Diamond
Ruby
Opal
Peridot
Turquoise

I brought precious Alphadots from planet Cryz Tahl to trade for gemstones from Earth, but I dropped them all over this page. How many can you find?

Color the Birthstones

Garnet—purplish red
Amethyst—purple
Aquamarine—greenish blue
Diamond—white
Emerald—green
Pearl—white

Ruby—red
Peridot—light green
Sapphire—blue
Opal—blue, and green and white
Topaz—orangish yellow
Turquoise—light blue

Standards Link Reading Comprehension: Follow Written Directions. Matching.

Where can you always find diamonds?

ANSWER: In a deck of cards.

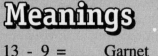 **Birthstones**

Birthstone Meanings

Each birthstone has a special meaning. To find out, do each math problem, put your answer on the line next to each gem, and then find the answer in the list on the right.

13 - 9 = ____ Garnet
7 - 2 = ____ Amethyst
4 + 3 = ____ Aquamarine
4 + 4 = ____ Diamond
15 - 6 = ____ Emerald
16 - 5 = ____ Pearl

18 - 16 = ____ Ruby
9 - 6 = ____ Peridot
11 - 10 = ____ Sapphire
2 + 4 = ____ Opal
8 + 2 = ____ Topaz
16 - 4 = ____ Turquoise

1. Good thinking
2. Contentment
3. Married happiness
4. Dependability
5. Sincerity
6. Hope
7. Courage
8. Innocence
9. Love
10. Loyalty
11. Health
12. Success

Standards Link Health: Connect Personal Characteristics that Contribute to Positive Self-esteem. Math: Calculate Sums and Differences.

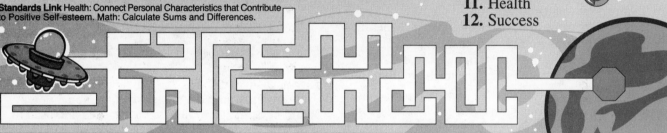

Birthstone Survey

| My birthstone is: |
| My friend's birthstone is: |
| My teacher's birthstone is: |
| My pet's birthstone is: |

Family-member birthstones:

Name	Birthstone

Standards Link Language Arts: Research; Locate Information Through Interview and Investigation.

Double Double Word Search

Find the words in the puzzle, then in the Kid Scoop stories and activities.

B	I	R	G	A	R	N	E	T	S
A	P	E	R	I	D	O	T	U	D
M	T	R	H	S	E	T	O	R	I
E	N	I	R	A	M	A	U	Q	A
T	Y	H	N	L	E	E	Z	U	M
H	B	P	E	A	R	L	A	O	O
Y	U	P	S	P	A	Q	P	I	N
S	R	A	U	O	L	I	O	S	D
T	M	S	N	O	D	A	T	E	T

AQUAMARINE   RUBY
GARNET   PERIDOT
AMETHYST   SAPPHIRE
DIAMOND   OPAL
EMERALD   TOPAZ
PEARL   TURQUOISE

Standards Link Language Arts: Spelling: Letter Sequencing; Reading: Vocabulary Development: Recognize Identical Words.

Name_____ Date _____

What are the three R's?
And, how can they save the Earth?

Every day the average kid makes about 3 pounds of trash, or more! That adds up to more than 1,000 pounds of trash a year!

Nearly all of this trash ends up in landfills. But landfills are filling up and we are running out of places to put trash.

Many experts agree that Americans must do something about the trash problem. They say that the problem is going to get worse. Is there anything we can do?

The three R's can help to beat the trash problem!

Hi, kids! Mother Earth here, asking for your help in making me a happier, healthier planet. Always remember the three Rs!

REDUCE!

We can make less trash. Buy things that don't use a lot of packaging.

Watch your weight!

One morning, weigh an empty trash can in your kitchen. Weigh it again at the end of the day. How many pounds of trash does your family toss in one day? See if your family can lose "waste weight" in a week.

Which makes less trash?

Make juice from frozen concentrate and take it to school in a reusable plastic container.

Trash per week:

Take a boxed juice in your school lunch.

Trash per week:

Standards Link Earth Science: Students Understand Ways to Conserve Resources.

REUSE!

We can change trash into something useful. Before you toss anything into the trash can, think about how it could be used again. Jars can be washed and used to store things. Plastic butter tubs can be used to pack food for lunches. Some trash can be turned into toys!

The Scoop!

Have some fun while protecting our planet with the Scoop Game! Wash empty plastic milk jugs and follow the directions to make your scoops.

1. To make a scoop, cut away the bottom and one side of a plastic milk jug as shown.   Cut here

2. Use the scoops to toss a ball back and forth. See who can catch the ball most often in one minute!

Plastic Power Bowling

1. Save six or more plastic bottles—soda, milk, laundry soap, dishwashing liquid, etc.

2. Clean bottles thoroughly and remove the labels.

3. Place the bottles in a triangle shape.

4. See how many you and your friends can knock down with a medium-sized ball.

Standards Link Reading Comprehension: Students Follow Multiple-step Directions.

Why are garbage men unhappy?

ANSWER: Because they are always down in the dumps.

Name_____ Date _____

RECYCLE!

If the Pilgrims had used aluminum cans at the first Thanksgiving, those cans would still be around today. An important way to reduce trash in landfills is to recycle it! Contact your local waste management company to find out what you can recycle.

This symbol on a product's packaging tells you that it can be recycled. Also, try to buy products that say "Made from Recycled Materials" on the packaging.

Follow each path to find out what new products can be made from different kinds of trash.

Standards Link Earth Science: Students Identify Different Resources and Classify Them as Renewable and Non-renewable.

▷▷▷▷▷ EARTH ALERT FACTS ◁◁◁◁◁

Unscramble the words in CAPITAL letters to discover some fascinating facts about waste.

Americans open their ①ERGARFROTIRE an average of 22 times a day. You can save ②YENREG by making fewer trips to the ③DIFREG and by keeping the ④ODOR open for only a few seconds.

①GAGCAPNIK materials make up about 30% of the trash in ②FALNLIDSL.

Making new ①SAGLS from old ②SLAGS containers is ③REGYEN efficient. The ④RYGNEE saved by recycling one ⑤LASGS ⑥TOBLET could run your TV set for three hours.

Standards Link Science: Students Understand Ways to Conserve Resources.

Find the words in the puzzle, then in the Kid Scoop stories and activities.

```
M  I  N  U  T  E  H  T  O  M
T  M  W  R  W  S  R  L  C  E
E  I  E  A  E  A  E  L  I  L
N  L  C  C  S  C  A  A  T  B
A  K  A  H  U  T  Y  B  S  O
L  L  N  D  E  W  E  C  A  R
P  E  E  A  R  T  H  A  L  P
L  R  L  S  W  B  V  S  P  E
E  S  L  L  I  F  D  N  A  L
```

REDUCE	WASTE
RECYCLE	PLANET
REUSE	PLACES
TRASH	PROBLEM
PLASTIC	MINUTE
LANDFILLS	MILK
EARTH	BALL
ALERT	

Standards Link Language Arts: Spelling: Letter Sequencing; Reading: Vocabulary Development: Recognize Identical Words.

Name_____ Date _____

Kid Scoop® Daylight Saving Time

Spring Forward!

Did you know sunflowers turn their heads to follow the sun? People have also discovered a simple way to get more from the sun.

Some parts of the world save energy and enjoy sunny summer evenings by turning clocks an hour forward in the spring. **It's called daylight saving time.**

Find the two identical sunflowers.

Standards Link Scientific Investigation: Find Similarities and Differences in Common Objects.

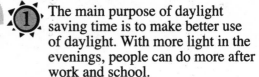

Why Daylight Saving Time?

1. The main purpose of daylight saving time is to make better use of daylight. With more light in the evenings, people can do more after work and school.

2. Daylight saving time also saves energy. A good percentage of electricity consumed by lighting and appliances occurs in the evening when families are home.

3. There is a small public health benefit to daylight saving time. According to studies in the U.S. and Britain, the risk of pedestrians getting hit by a car is four times less during daylight than after dark.

Standards Link Social Science: Students Correctly Apply Terms Related to Time; Identify and Interpret Multiple Effects of Events.

It's All in the Timing!

Use the time zone map on the next page to help you solve the following riddle. Draw the hands on the clock faces to show the time and label each zone.

Jerry lives in California and eats lunch at noon. At the same time, his cousin Jennifer in Maine plays basketball. Three hours later, her pen pal Julie in eastern Texas sets the table for dinner. Her cousin Jody in Utah is at swimming lessons.

1 TIME ZONE:

2 TIME ZONE:

3 TIME ZONE:

4 TIME ZONE:

What do you get when you cross an alarm clock and a chicken?

ANSWER: An alarm cluck!

Name_____ Date _____

Changing Time

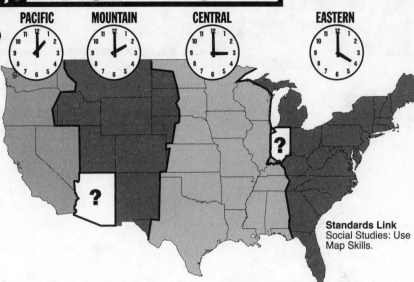

PACIFIC · MOUNTAIN · CENTRAL · EASTERN

Daylight saving time begins for most of the United States on the first Sunday of April. In spring, clocks are changed at 2:00 a.m. and spring forward to 3:00 a.m. On the last Sunday in October at 2:00 a.m., clocks fall back to 1:00 a.m.

Daylight saving time, for the mainland U.S., is NOT observed in the Eastern time zone portion of the state of Indiana, or the state of Arizona.*

Standards Link Math: Measurement; Understand Time.

Standards Link
Social Studies: Use
Map Skills.

Read "Changing Time" to identify the two states that do not entirely observe daylight saving time.

* The exception in Arizona is the Navajo Indian Reservation, which does observe daylight saving time because of the size of the Navajo Nation and its location in three states.

GREAT IDEA!

When you set your clocks at daylight saving time, replace the batteries in your smoke detectors, too!

Who Invented Daylight Saving Time?

To shed light on the name of the early American inventor and statesman that came up with the idea of daylight saving time, use your ABCs! Look at the letter above each box. Write the letter that comes after each letter in the box below it.

Example:

A	B	C
B	C	D

A D M
☐ ☐ ☐

E Q Z M J K H M
☐ ☐ ☐ ☐ ☐ ☐ ☐ ☐

Standards Link Reading Comprehension: Follow Simple Written Directions.

Double Double Word Search

Find the words in the puzzle, then in the Kid Scoop stories and activities.

S	P	S	K	C	O	L	C	S	O
R	I	H	R	N	G	F	T	T	R
G	W	E	O	A	G	A	E	H	A
N	R	D	W	N	T	T	O	G	N
I	S	E	I	E	A	U	D	I	A
R	D	V	M	E	R	F	A	L	L
P	A	P	R	I	L	F	A	Y	O
S	E	C	L	L	T	B	A	A	G
C	H	T	L	A	E	H	K	D	E

DAYLIGHT	APRIL
SAVING	HEADS
TIME	HOUR
SPRING	SHED
FALL	STATE
CLOCKS	HEALTH
WORK	

Standards Link Language Arts: Spelling: Letter Sequencing; Reading: Vocabulary Development: Recognize Identical Words.

Name_____ Date _____

Wild and Crazy Moms!

Which animal would you like to be **your** mom?

Motherhood means different things to different animals. Read about how these animal mothers care, or don't care, for their young. Which animal mother would you like to have?

FINISH

Silly Sheep
It is not uncommon for a sheep to simply abandon its lamb. Farmers often have to bottle-feed lambs.

Help the little lost sheep find the farmer with the bottle.

START

Donkey Devotion
Donkey mothers may be the most devoted of all. They will not let any other animal come between them and their babies. Even if a curious little kitten comes close, a donkey mom will chase it away.

Strange Reflection
Find the differences between the mother donkey and its foal and their reflection in the pond.

Standards Link Visual Discrimination: Finding Similarities and Differences in Common Objects.

EGGS-tra Fun
Use the numbers **4,5,6,7,8,9.**

Make the top row of eggs equal **6.**

Make the sum of the middle row of eggs equal **16.**

Make the sum of the bottom row equal **17.**

Standards Link Math: Find the Sum of Whole Numbers to 20; Students Use Strategies, Skills, and Concepts in Finding Solutions.

Animal Adoptions

Sometimes a goat will abandon its kid. Usually a farmer does not have to bottle-feed the little critter because another nanny goat will step in and adopt it.

Adoptions can also be seen in the chicken coop. Some hens will sit on any eggs that happen to be around.

Standards Link Science: Different Animals Inhabit the Earth, Reproduce, and Adapt in Different Ways to Survive.

What do hippopotamuses have that no other animals have?

ANSWER: Baby hippopotamuses.

Kid Scoop — Animal Moms

Underwater Moms

Frogs and fish moms generally lay their eggs and forget about them. Fortunately, once the eggs hatch, the tiny tadpoles and baby fish can survive on their own. In fact, one of the predators they have to watch out for is their own mom! Find eight things in the pond that don't belong.

Standards Link Science: Different Animals Reproduce and Adapt in Different Ways to Survive; Classify Objects.

Tadpole Backpack

The mother Surinam toad cares for its eggs in one of the strangest ways. As the mother toad lays eggs, the male presses them one by one into the soft skin on the mother's back. After a while, each egg sinks into a little pocket that forms on the mother's back. Then a covering of skin grows over the pocket. The baby toads hatch and develop in these little pockets. A few weeks later, the mother rubs her back and the little toads swim free.

What did the mother Surinam toad say to her kids?

Unscramble the answer:
"ETG FOF YM AKBC!"

Standards Link Science: Survival Strategies.

Double Double Word Search

Find the words in the puzzle, then in the Kid Scoop stories and activities.

C	H	I	C	K	E	N	O	R	F
H	T	G	M	D	L	A	M	B	I
A	A	F	R	O	G	S	E	O	S
S	D	A	H	N	M	O	U	T	H
E	P	R	A	K	G	S	P	T	U
Y	O	M	T	E	I	H	O	L	O
O	L	E	C	Y	F	E	N	E	M
U	E	R	H	K	R	E	G	G	S
P	S	A	M	B	C	P	O	N	D

FARMER   TADPOLES
EGGS   FISH
DONKEY   LAMB
MOMS   POND
SHEEP   CHICKEN
FROGS   CHASE
BOTTLE   HATCH

Standards Link Language Arts: Spelling: Letter Sequencing; Reading: Vocabulary Development: Recognize Identical Words.

Name_____   Date _____

TALES OF SUNKEN TREASURE!

A Sunken City

In the 1600s, Port Royal, Jamaica, was one of the busiest seaports in the Caribbean. It was home to merchants, missionaries, smugglers, and pirates.

In 1692 an earthquake hit the city. Much of it sank 65 feet (20 meters) below sea level. For hundreds of years, sand and mud covered the city. Many treasure seekers tried to find the sunken city and failed.

Then, in 1965, a diver named Robert Marx used modern equipment to dig under the layers of mud and found the lost city. He was not looking for treasure, but find it he did!

Thousands of coins were found —perhaps lost pirate treasure.

ABC Treasure Hunt

Take a trip under the deep blue sea and look for treasures from A to Z. Can you find each letter of the alphabet hidden in the picture?

Standards Link Decoding; Match All Consonants and Vowel Sounds to Appropriate Letters.

Sunken Ships

Long ago, Spanish ships full of treasure sailed the seas. Sometimes these ships sank, leaving tons of treasure on the sea floor. Search the sea floor for seven coins with letters on them. Unscramble the letters to find out what these ships were called!

A Spanish treasure ship was called a

____ ____ ____ ____ ____ ____ ____ .

Standards Link Spelling: Spell Independently Combining Letters to Form Words; Vocabulary Development.

What's the difference between a PIRATE and a FARMER?

ANSWER: A farmer treasures his berries. A pirate buries his treasures.

Name_____ Date _____

Shark Alert

Diving for the lost city of Port Royal is dangerous. Divers must watch out for sharks.

Do all sharks look the same? No sirree! Circle five ways the two sharks are different.

Standards Link Scientific Investigation: Find Similarities and Differences in Common Objects.

Uncover the Unlikely

Well, shiver me timbers! There are two land animals hiding in the Sunken Treasure picture. Can you find them?

Standards Link
Visual Discrimination.

Treasure Hunter Clues

Divers looking for sunken treasure do not look for the hulls of sunken ships. Wooden hulls rot after hundreds of years under water.

Treasure hunters look instead for lumps that could be the remains of metal parts of a ship: cannons, anchors, tools, and ballast. Sometimes, even these are hard to see, as most of them have been encrusted with sand and shells.

Sunken SOMETHING

Some say that in 1876, *something* carrying millions of dollars of gold crashed and fell into the Ashtabula River in Ohio. Many have tried to find the buried bullion, but to date no one has. Do you think it is really there? Or is it a legend?

To find out what crashed, color each space with one dot BLACK, and color each space with two dots BLUE.

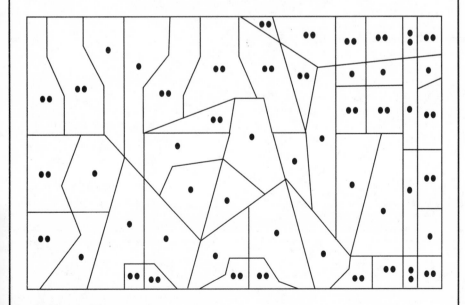

Standards Link Physical Education: Eye Hand Coordination.

Double Double Word Search

Find the words in the puzzle, then in the Kid Scoop stories and activities.

T	A	L	D	N	A	S	E	T	S
O	E	L	Y	R	E	T	S	Y	M
F	O	R	S	U	R	O	U	T	K
G	N	S	U	E	L	D	N	I	R
K	E	H	V	S	U	N	K	C	A
A	C	I	A	M	A	J	E	T	H
R	D	P	I	R	T	E	N	E	S
S	M	U	G	G	L	E	R	S	A
S	L	A	Y	O	R	U	R	T	E

SUNKEN	LOST
TREASURE	CITY
JAMAICA	SAND
SMUGGLERS	ROYAL
SHIP	SHARK
DIVER	MUD
GOLD	TRIP

Standards Link Language Arts: Spelling: Letter Sequencing; Reading: Vocabulary Development: Recognize Identical Words.

Name_____ Date _____

Kid Scoop® Pink Dolphins

Pink Dolphins?

A shy and unusual dolphin species lives in the fresh water of the Amazon River of South America. They are called pink dolphins because many of them have a pinkish color of skin.

Amazon River

South America

The pink dolphin looks very different from the ocean-dwelling dolphin many of us are familiar with. The ocean dolphin is built for speed. It needs to be fast to cover large distances, catch prey, and escape danger.

The pink dolphin is built to navigate the tree-jammed, shallow waters of the Amazon River, where it must be able to bend its body around obstacles. In fact, it can touch its nose to its tail! It has a very low dorsal fin, a long tubular snout, and quite a round head. It also has large front flippers. The pink river dolphin has been known to crawl on land using its large front flippers.

Kid Scoop Scientist

How many differences can you find between the pink river dolphin and the ocean dolphin? Read about the pink dolphins to see if you found them all.

Standards Link Visual Discrimination: Observing Similarities and Differences in Common Objects.

Standards Link Science: Animals Have Different Features that Help Them Thrive in Different Environments.

Pink River Dolphin

Ocean Dolphin

Cetacean Family

Did you know dolphins are a kind of whale? The largest dolphin is even called a whale. It is the killer whale. Whales, dolphins, and porpoises are known as **cetaceans** (suy TAY shuhns). Cetaceans bear live young and the babies nurse on the mother's milk. They live entirely in the water and breathe air through lungs.

Help the baby pink river dolphin find her way through the submerged tree roots to her mom.

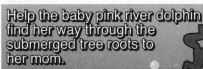

Standards Link Language Arts: Reading Comprehension; Physical Education: Eye Hand Coordination.

Why do they say that dolphins talk a lot?

ANSWER: Because dolphins are always spouting off.

Name_____ Date _____

Oldest Living Whale

When you look at a pink river dolphin, you are seeing what prehistoric whales looked like, after they lost their legs and hooves. *Legs and hooves?* Yes, whales were once land-dwelling animals!

Some scientists believe these landlubber whales looked a bit like small dogs and were related to cows, sheep, and pigs. Over time their arms became flippers, their legs disappeared, and their tails grew larger and widened to form flukes. Today, whale flippers contain the bones of five fingers, like our hands.

Draw what you think prehistoric whales might have looked like when they had legs and hooves. Read the description in "Oldest Living Whale" for ideas.

Standards Link Reading Comprehension: Sequencing Events in a Narrative.

Amazon Dolphin Legend

In the legends of the people who live along the Amazon, the pink dolphin is magical and can transform itself from dolphin to human. When a pink dolphin raises its round, pink head out of the muddy Amazon River water, it looks a bit like the head of a human. Some say that if you go to a dance and fall in love with a handsome stranger, beware that you may have fallen in love with a pink dolphin posing as a person.

Find the pink dolphin that's different.

Standards Link Language Arts: Literary Response & Analysis: Comprehend Basic Plots of Legends.

Double Double Word Search

Find the words in the puzzle, then in the Kid Scoop stories and activities.

R	O	C	E	A	N	M	A	S	G
L	I	A	T	T	D	I	G	C	A
L	A	V	U	I	O	E	M	A	L
O	A	O	E	T	L	U	N	G	S
H	N	E	N	R	P	I	N	K	E
S	E	V	O	O	H	O	F	A	L
K	M	A	S	Z	I	I	O	N	A
I	R	I	E	V	N	A	M	U	H
N	E	R	T	S	R	E	T	A	W

RIVER	HUMAN
DOLPHIN	WHALES
PINK	FINS
LEGS	LUNGS
HOOVES	WATERS
SNOUT	NOSE
OCEAN	TAIL
SKIN	

Standards Link Language Arts: Spelling: Letter Sequencing; Reading: Vocabulary Development: Recognize Identical Words.

Kid Scoop® Animal Dads

Animal Dads

Most animals never even see their parents! Insects, fish, amphibians, and other animals that hatch from eggs often start life completely alone.

A lot of animals are raised by their mothers. But in some surprising cases, it is the **dads** who are in charge.

Standards Link Science: Different Animals Have Features that Help Them Reproduce and Thrive in Different Environments.

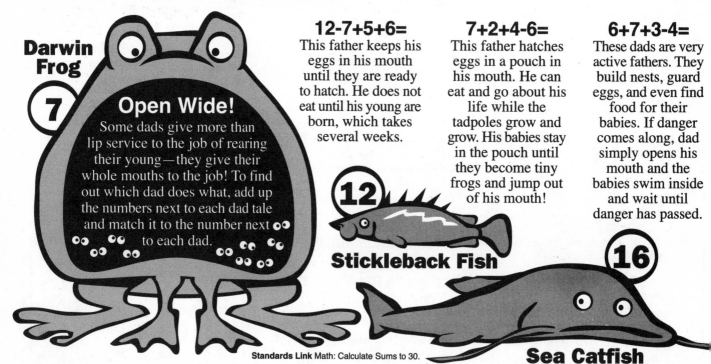

Darwin Frog

7

Open Wide!

Some dads give more than lip service to the job of rearing their young—they give their whole mouths to the job! To find out which dad does what, add up the numbers next to each dad tale and match it to the number next to each dad.

$12-7+5+6=$
This father keeps his eggs in his mouth until they are ready to hatch. He does not eat until his young are born, which takes several weeks.

$7+2+4-6=$
This father hatches eggs in a pouch in his mouth. He can eat and go about his life while the tadpoles grow and grow. His babies stay in the pouch until they become tiny frogs and jump out of his mouth!

$6+7+3-4=$
These dads are very active fathers. They build nests, guard eggs, and even find food for their babies. If danger comes along, dad simply opens his mouth and the babies swim inside and wait until danger has passed.

12

Stickleback Fish

16

Sea Catfish

Standards Link Math: Calculate Sums to 30.

Soggy Dad

The father Namaqua Sand Grouse of Africa's Kalahari Desert flies as far as 50 miles a day in order to soak himself in water and return to his nest, where his chicks drink from his feathers! **Help the sand grouse find his nest.**

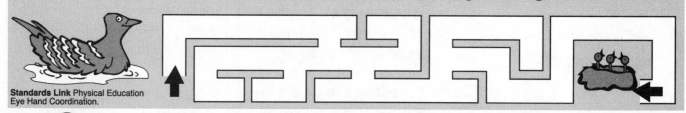

Standards Link Physical Education Eye Hand Coordination.

Who is bigger: Mr. Bigger or Mr. Bigger's baby?

ANSWER: The baby is a little Bigger.

Kid Scoop® Animal Dads

Now THAT is baby-sitting!

Can you imagine sitting in one place for nine weeks? That is what the father emperor penguin does. After the mom lays an egg, father penguin holds it on his feet, keeping it warm under a special feather flap. He holds that egg for nine weeks! During this time he doesn't eat a thing. A father penguin can lose about 25 pounds while waiting for the baby to hatch. After the baby hatches, the mom and dad take turns feeding and caring for their downy youngster.

Standards Link Reading Comprehension: Follow Simple Directions; Visual Discrimination.

What has changed in nine weeks? Find five or more differences.

What three letters make a man of a boy? A-G-E.

A Dad That Gives Birth?

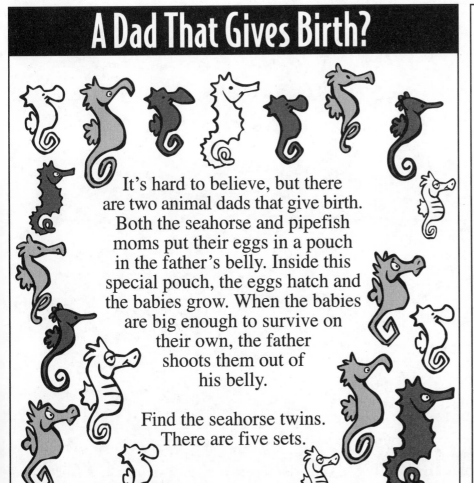

It's hard to believe, but there are two animal dads that give birth. Both the seahorse and pipefish moms put their eggs in a pouch in the father's belly. Inside this special pouch, the eggs hatch and the babies grow. When the babies are big enough to survive on their own, the father shoots them out of his belly.

Find the seahorse twins. There are five sets.

Standards Link Scientific Investigation: Identify Similarities and Differences in Common Objects.

Double Double Word Search

Find the words in the puzzle, then in the Kid Scoop stories and activities.

F	L	A	P	S	S	P	E	A	C
A	D	K	D	T	B	E	L	L	Y
Y	H	A	T	C	H	N	G	F	I
O	D	L	R	S	C	G	R	G	H
U	D	A	R	W	H	U	O	W	S
N	I	H	N	F	I	I	W	R	O
G	U	A	R	D	C	N	E	S	T
W	A	R	M	G	K	T	A	D	P
O	L	I	E	S	S	B	A	B	Y

KALAHARI   YOUNG
DARWIN   EGGS
HATCH   BELLY
PENGUIN   DADS
CHICKS   GROW
GUARD   BABY
WARM   FLAP
NEST

Standards Link Language Arts: Spelling: Letter Sequencing; Reading: Vocabulary Development: Recognize Identical Words.

Name_____ Date _____

Sunburn

Ouch!!!

Hot fun in the summertime can be painful! Too much fun in the sun can burn your skin.

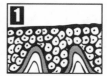 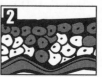 

How does the sun burn skin?

1. Normal skin.
2. Cells that get too much sunlight swell and fill with blood.
3. This turns skin red and makes it hurt.

Standards Link Science: People Have Structures that Serve Different Functions.

To burn or not to burn?

Everybody has tiny grains of color called **melanin** in their skin.

Melanin grains are like a screen. They protect the body from the burning rays of sunlight. Everybody's skin makes melanin. Melanin grains are brown. When your skin is exposed to the sun, it makes more melanin. That is why your skin gets darker when you play in the sunshine.

Tanya has a lot of melanin in her skin. Andy and Melody have a little. Amy has very little. Some parts of Amy's body make more melanin than others. These dark spots are called freckles.

Everybody needs to protect their skin from the sun. Even people with lots of melanin will burn. Their skin won't burn as fast as Amy's, but it *will* burn.

Standards Link Science: People Have Features that Help Them Thrive in Different Environments.

Tanya   Melody   Andy   Amy

Lifesaver Letters

What should you look for when you are getting too much sun? Cross out every letter that is printed twice on the inner tube. The five letters left spell your answer!

VBSRMHVMROAYKYBDOKE

Standards Link Reading Comprehension: Follow Simple Directions; Identify Common Sight Words.

What does the sun do when it gets tired?

ANSWER: It sets awhile.

60

Independent Activity Pages for Reading

Scholastic

Kid Scoop Sunburn

What is hiding at the beach?

banana	bat	watermelon	bowling ball	moon
octopus	dolphin	ice cream	car	

Standards Link: Visual discrimination.

How many things on this page start with the letter S?

When are you most likely to dream about going away for the summer? When you're asleep.

Find 16 little sticks and try this puzzle. Lay out the sticks like Amy did. Can you make 5 squares by moving only 2 sticks?

Standards Link Math: Problem Solving: Make a Model to Solve a Puzzle.

Close-ups

Andy took pictures at the beach. He got really close to things. Can you figure out what he was photographing? They are in the picture of Tanya, Melody, and Amy.

SPF 30

Standards Link Language Arts: Generalizing from Detail.

Double Double Word Search

Find the words in the puzzle, then in the Kid Scoop stories and activities.

L	S	U	R	A	Y	S	C	D	N
B	I	C	N	D	B	U	O	A	R
R	N	F	O	Y	O	U	O	R	M
O	R	B	E	A	C	H	L	K	E
W	S	U	N	S	H	I	N	E	L
N	P	S	K	K	A	I	N	R	A
H	O	T	I	I	E	V	T	H	N
U	T	T	I	N	Y	R	E	T	I
S	S	H	U	R	T	B	U	R	N

BURN	BODY
LIFESAVER	SPOTS
SKIN	HOT
MELANIN	RAYS
SUNSHINE	BROWN
DARKER	TINY
BEACH	HURT

Standards Link Language Arts: Spelling: Letter Sequencing; Reading: Vocabulary Development: Recognize Identical Words.

Answers

Page 5
▶ Awesome Apples

▶ Scrambled A's: 30

Page 6
▶ Alpaca Facts: 22, 20, 36, 150

Page 7
▶ Famous Fur

Page 8
▶ Spot the Backpack Blunders

Page 9
▶ What's in Silly Sam's Backpack?

Page 11
▶ Silly Signing: A SLOWPOKE

Page 12
▶ How big is a snowy owl?: MICROWAVE OVEN, TEACHER'S DESK, HOUSE CAT, BASEBALL BAT, TENNIS RACKET

▶ Why White?: LEOPARD, DEER, TIGER

Page 13
▶ The Eyes Have It

Page 15
▶ If It Moves, It's Mother: DOG, A BALL, AND A BLOCK OF WOOD

Page 16
▶ Which two bats are the same?: SECOND FROM RIGHT, FOURTH FROM RIGHT

Page 17
▶ Clean Kids: WASH WITH SOAP AND WATER

Page 18
▶ 1: 1 and 4; 2: 1 and 3; 3: 1, 2 and 4 / 3 and 5; 4: 1 and 4

Page 19
▶ Dino Duos

▶ Name That Dinosaur: SAUROPODS—TRICERATOPS, STEGOSAURUS/ THERAPODS—TYRANNOSAURUS REX

Page 20
▶ First Children's Book Week Poster: MORE BOOKS IN THE HOME

▶ Secret Decoder

Page 21
▶ Picture Puzzle: FUEL YOUR MIND

Page 22
▶ Border: A PENNY SAVED IS A PENNY EARNED

Page 23
▶ Heaviest Pumpkin Contest: PUMPKIN ON THE LEFT

Page 25
▶ Ducky Difference: BOTTOM LEFT

Page 27
▶ Find the hidden pictures

▶ Find the stamp that is different: TOP RIGHT

▶ Which stamp comes next?

Page 28
▶ How Old Is Your Christmas Tree?: MY CHRISTMAS TREE SURVIVED A FIRE IN 1991. MY TREE WAS PLANTED IN 1985. 1997 WAS A GOOD GROWING YEAR

Page 29
▶ Read the Rings

	Age of the tree	Year tree was cut down	Year tree was planted
LIVING TREE	29	2000	1972
DR. SAPLING'S CHRISTMAS TREE	16	2000	1985
LOG FROM CABIN	27	1992	1966

Page 30
▶ What's at the end of the rainbow?: PEACE

Page 33
▶ Help Paula Predict the Weather: WESTOWN

◆ Snowman Match Game: TOP RIGHT, BOTTOM MIDDLE

Page 34
▶ The Power of the Pen

Page 35
▶ Puzzling Pens

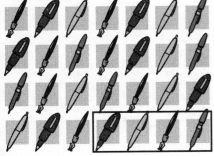

Page 37
▶ Heart Smart Treasure Puzzle: 1-N; 2-P; 3-R; 4-U; 5-X; 6-D; 7-1; 8-C; 9-H

▶ Pulse Puzzle: MOUSE 700; CHILD 120; ADULT 90; ELEPHANT 25

Page 38
▶ Scientists' notebook

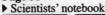

Page 39
▶ Mammoth Math: 100,000 YEARS; 7 TONS; 47 YEARS OLD; 12 HAIR DRIERS

▶ Melting Mix-up: PENCIL, GRAPES, SAW, PAINT BRUSH, CHRISTMAS TREE, DOLPHIN, SNAIL

Page 40
▶ Where Did They Go?: BLUE TEAM— NOME; RED TEAM—IDITAROD; YELLOW TEAM—FAIRBANKS

▶ The Iditarod Trail: THE TRAIL IS 1,100 MILES LONG. THE TRAIL CROSSES OVER 2 MOUNTAIN RANGES AND TAKES FROM 9 TO 21 DAYS DEPENDING ON THE WEATHER

Page 41
▶ Husky Heroes: TOP MIDDLE, BOTTOM RIGHT

Page 42
▶ Can you find the four-leaf clover?

Page 45
▶ Crazy Cockpit

Page 43
▶ Where's Betty's Bovine?: TOP RIGHT

Page 44
▶ Transatlantic Trip: IRELAND

Page 46
▶ Alphadots: 21

Page 49
▶ Earth Alert Facts: 1: REFRIGERATOR; 2: ENERGY; 3: FRIDGE; 4; DOOR

▶ 1: PACKAGING, 2: LANDFILLS

▶ 1: GLASS, 2: GLASS, 3: ENERGY, 4: ENERGY, 5: GLASS, 6: BOTTLE

Page 50
▶ Find the two identical sunflowers: FOURTH FROM RIGHT, SIXTH FROM RIGHT

▶ It's All in the Timing: 1. JENNIFER, EASTERN, 3:00. 2. JERRY, PACIFIC 12:00. 3. JULIE, CENTRAL, 5:00. 4. JODY, MOUNTAIN, 4:00

Page 51
▶ Who Invented Daylight Saving Time?: BEN FRANKLIN

Page 52
▶ Eggs-tra Fun: TOP ROW: 6, MIDDLE ROW: 97, BOTTOM ROW: 845

Page 53
▶ Underwater Moms: WHISTLE, HOT DOG, HAT, AIRPLANE, SHOE, TOOTHBRUSH, BOWLING BALL, PIG

▶ Tadpole Backpack: "GET OFF MY BACK!"

Page 54
▶ A Spanish treasure ship was called a GALLEON

Page 54
▶ ABC Treasure Hunt: ○ = ALPHABET

Page 55
▶ Uncover the Unlikely: □ = Land animals

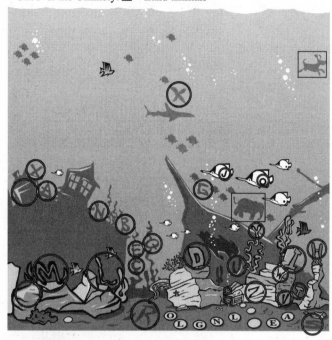

▶ Sunken Something

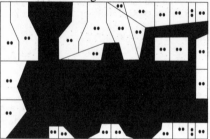

Page 57
▶ Amazon Dolphin Legend: BOTTOM DOLPHIN, BECAUSE OF SHAPE OF BEAK

Page 58
▶ Animal Dads: 12-7+5+6=SEA CAT FISH: 7+2+4-6=DARWIN FROG: 6+7+3-4=STICKLEBACK FISH

Page 59
▶ Now THAT is baby-sitting?

▶ Find the seahorse twins

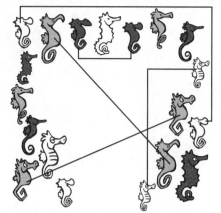

Page 60
▶ Lifesaver Letters: SHADE

Page 61
▶ ○ = What is hiding at the beach?

▶ □ = Close-ups

▶ Can you make 5 squares by moving only 2 sticks?